RECIPES FOR ENCHANTMENT

ENCHANTMENT

The Secret Ingredient is YOU!

RECIPES FOR ENCHANTMENT

ENCHANTMENT

The Secret Ingredient is YOU!

BY DR. BARBARA BECKER HOLSTEIN

ISBN: 1-58820-362-X

THE ENCHANTED SELF® is a registered trademark of
Barbara Becker Holstein

1stBooks – rev. 12/14/00

ENDORSEMENTS
RECIPES FOR ENCHANTMENT
The Secret Ingredient is YOU!

This heartwarming collection of stories reminds us that we have only to look at what's right in front of us to experience life's most beautiful and sacred moments. **RECIPES FOR ENCHANTMENT, The Secret Ingredient is YOU!** offers the reader inspiration *and* a hands-on opportunity to explore the uniqueness of one's own life, ultimately realizing that "being you is the most fabulous adventure of all!"

> ~~ **Jennifer Read Hawthorne**, author of
> *A Second Chicken Soup for the Woman's Soul, 101 More Stories to Open the Hearts and Rekindle the Spirits of Women*

Dr. Barbara Holstein's new book, **RECIPES FOR ENCHANTMENT, The Secret Ingredient is You!**, is an inspirational book of beautifully told stories followed by journaling activities, that encourage hope, optimism and well being. Pick up the book when you could use a little jolt of human warmth and positivity and, guaranteed, you will smile and your heart will feel gladdened. This book reminds us all to recognize the opportunities that come our way daily to bring more pleasure and joy into our own lives and into the lives of others.

~~**Dr. Stella Resnick, Ph.D.,** is a clinical psychologist and psychotherapist in private practice in Los Angeles and Ojai, California and the author of *The Pleasure Zone: Why We Resist Good Feelings & How to Let Go and Be Happy*

If you are ready for a great collection of inspiring, motivational stories that will mentor you as they inspire, start reading RECIPES FOR ENCHANTMENT. The stories stimulate while the follow up gives us a chance to process and grow. And if you're a therapist or coach, you'll love the great material RECIPES offers for your clients to work on as they work with you. RECIPES FOR ENCHANTMENT captures the spirit of mentoring.

~~**Ben Dean, Ph.D., Founder and CEO**
Mentor Coach ™

The wonder of these stories and the journaling activities that follow is they help you realize real happiness comes from following your dreams. RECIPES FOR ENCHANTMENT provides the formula for doing this. One of it's *secret* ingredients is that it works with what you have inside of yourself, helping you to get out there and live a life of "enchantment."

~~ **Jean Cirillo, Ph.D., Staff Psychologist**
Jennie Jones Show
Private Practice, Long Island, New York

IN TRIBUTE

This book, RECIPES FOR ENCHANTMENT, THE SECRET INGREDIENT IS YOU!, is dedicated to my father, Dr. Harry Albert Becker (1912-1999). He taught me many valuable lessons, one of which was about the importance of never giving up. When I was in fourth grade, I was asked to give a talk in front of the class. I felt stymied and completely overwhelmed. My dad suggested that I relate Aesop's fable about the tortoise and the hare. What a clever idea! Not only did it give me the opportunity to teach my classmates about the value of persistence, but by rehearsing my recitation at home, I gradually internalized the fable's message, identifying with the tortoise and proving to myself that I could succeed despite my initial doubts.

My dad also taught me to share learning whenever possible. To teach another was as important as learning itself. When I was twenty, I traveled in Europe and came home with many stories about visiting West Germany and the Berlin Wall. He encouraged me to write these stories and submit them to our local newspaper, "The Norwalk Hour," so that our neighbors could have a first-hand opportunity to learn about what was happening abroad.

My father taught me too that positive actions can lead to positive change. He was not only among those who founded Connecticut's first two-year college, Norwalk Community College, which opened its doors in the 1960s, but also served as its first president. He was prescient in his understanding that public two-year institutions would prove to be the gateway through which thousands of people could gain access to higher education.

Finally, he taught me that perspiration is more important than inspiration in finalizing a project. He achieved a difficult balance – he was able to dream, yet he had the courage to mobilize his convictions to create positive change in the world.

For all these reasons, RECIPES FOR ENCHANTMENT, with its emphasis on positive thoughts, feelings and actions, is a reflection of what I had learned from my father. To work on this book during my year of mourning was a blessing. It provided me with a dual opportunity to stay very close to my dad while doing exactly what he would have wished – to find ways to translate my private thoughts into productive action in the world.

This book contains many special treats, including two delightful stories written by his sweetheart, my beloved mother, Bernice Becker. I have also incorporated many of my own reflections, memories and stories about my life, some of which relate to my growing up. There are stories that describe my tribal connections to Judaism. In addition, I have included stories from readers of THE ENCHANTED SELF newsletter. This gives me great satisfaction. I am thankful that THE ENCHANTED SELF concepts have traveled around the world.

So thank you, Daddy, for giving me life, lessons, love, and a sense of purpose. Thanks too for teaching me to ride my two-wheel bicycle when I was four. You got me started, and it's been a great ride!

Love, Barbara - May 10, 2000

✕

RECIPES FOR ENCHANTMENT
The Secret Ingredient Is YOU!

❀ ❀ ❀ ❀ ❀ ❀ ❀ ❀

Introduction

❀ ❀ ❀

Baking – Loaves of Love
Believing – Joey Figures it Out
Belonging – When Saturday Was Really Saturday
Caring – Doggy Day Care
Completing – Mr. Diamond's Last Trip Through Elizabeth
Connecting – Sally's Family Ties
Dancing – Dancing the Sardana
Discovering – The Mysterious Rabbi
Finding – There but By the Grace of God
Giving – The Universe Comes Through for Judy
Grieving – Memories, Grieving and Resolution
Harmonizing – The Peddler Who Came Through Town
Helping – The Japanese Ambassador
Laughing – How Could Timmie Disappear?
Learning – That Ain't Worth Nothin'
Living – Life at a Dharma Center: Challenging,
Rewarding, and Not Easy
Loving – Grandma Sadie's Blintzes
Mentoring – The Sweet Touch of Mr. Zuckerman
Praying – Learning from Little Children
Pretending – The Claydigger Finds a Diamond
Reminiscing – Not the Same Old Story

Renewing – The House My Great-Grandfather Built
Saving – A Soldier's Love for His Family
Savoring – Chocolate Circles of Love
Sharing – The Lady and the Biscuits
Singing – A Brighter Day
Surviving – The Rabbi Who Lived in the Woods
Trusting – The Hatpin
Visiting – Visiting the Matzo Factory
Waltzing – Grandfather Really Knew How to Dance!
Welcoming – A Familiar Friend
Wishing – A Vision

INTRODUCTION

I am Barbara Becker Holstein, psychologist, mother, wife, friend, child, and woman. Let me tell you more. After many years of study, I became a psychologist and developed a thriving private practice with my husband, Russell Holstein. But one day, I suddenly became aware that I had a small "hole" in my heart. It wasn't the kind of hole that requires surgery. It was the kind that heartache creates.

I began to realize that the hole had been there for a long time – in fact, since I was a little girl – and that the emptiness and pain that accompanied it could no longer be denied. It seemed to have grown out of the accumulated insults and disappointments I had sustained over many years.

Some of the pain was a direct result of the insulting messages, some subtle, some not, that society had given me and other women – a society that prizes external values over internal truths and that often views physical beauty as more important than inner wisdom; a society that dotes on youth, competition, money, and the outward trappings of success; a society in which I had grown up idolizing and identifying with movie stars rather than appreciating the other moms who lived on my block; a society that taught me not to accumulate cellulite on my thighs and encouraged me to marry young.

Over time I have also slowly come to recognize that many other women I know, both professionally and personally, seem to experience this emptiness too. With my clients, and even my own mother, I could identify particular ways in which they had all been diminished and demoralized. For example, my mother had been told by the patriarch of her family that she was beautiful but dumb, and her options were to be a saleslady in Filene's or a clerk. Needless to say, she didn't want to be either and chose instead to marry my father at 19.

One client told me how her husband deflated her every time she had a good idea by saying, "Well, that and 10 cents will get you a cup of coffee." Another client recalled that her husband had once turned to her and said, "You know, you're a very ineffectual and inefficient person." I have seen how the blows to these women's self-esteem not only penetrated their hearts but also took years of effort to repair – if indeed they could be fully repaired.

I wondered what other subtle, insidious, or mixed messages had contributed to the hole in my heart. Did they have to do with my definition of who I was? Did they have to do with the loss or discouragement of early talents, hopes, dreams? Did they have to do with living in a society that did not value sacred space and privacy? Did they have to do with the gradual erosion of a sense of joy or the difficulty of bringing enough joy into my daily life to give me pleasure?

My first book, *THE ENCHANTED SELF, A Positive Therapy*, tells at great length what I discovered about myself – how I became aware of the hole in my heart, and how I began the long journey that resulted not only in the healing of this hole, but also in my growing determination to bring more joy and happiness and a sense of well-being into others' lives as well as my own. I hope you will take the time to share my journey by reading *THE ENCHANTED SELF, A Positive Therapy*.

Indeed, the repair work had everything to do with reclaiming lost parts of myself, including my potential, interests, talents, and dreams, which had been stifled or disregarded by myself or others. It had everything to do with treasuring my own history, my own story, and seeing my life as a miraculous unfolding that had positive value for both myself and others. And it had everything to do with finally having the courage to redefine myself according to a definition that made me feel like a glorious and talented and wondrous woman with a full life, rather than struggling without motive and squelching definitions that people in my life, and society at large, had attempted to give me.

A turning point in repairing my heart and opening myself up to joy – which is certainly relevant to this book, *RECIPES FOR ENCHANTMENT, The Secret Ingredient is YOU!* – was the period in the early 1990's during which I interviewed a series of women who were not clients. These women, ranging in age from 35 to their 80s, gave *me* a gift, which I eventually called "enchantment."

I perceived that these women, even with such difficult lives, were able to live positively for the most part, at times seemingly by magic – to live lives of integrity while deriving pleasure, having fun, meeting challenges, seizing opportunities, and, in general, experiencing a sense of well-being. Even those women whose lives were interwoven with disappointment, pain, family difficulties, divorce, and loss of loved ones were able to do this.

I began to realize that we have been conditioned to perceive ourselves as women in more negative ways than necessary. How can I ever forget the excitement I felt while listening to a woman in her 70s tell me how she had been able to recapture so much joy after ending a bad marriage of 40 years! Her descriptions of herself folk dancing, rediscovering her love of playing the piano, managing her own money, becoming a nutritional guru of sorts, were all so life affirming. She even negotiated successfully with her landlord so as not to receive a rent raise.

The psychologist and educator in me began to realize that we could practice positive states of well being and integrate them into our lives more and more often. I saw that I could teach my clients to see themselves in a more positive light, to recognize and focus on the best in themselves. I saw that I could do that with myself too. It became apparent to me that the more we women learn to negotiate and meet our needs more effectively, the more possibilities we will have to develop a sense of joy. The better we feel about ourselves, the more courage we will have to utilize ourselves effectively and develop our talents. This shift in perception of ourselves which encourages well-being, joy and a determined effort to live a life of purpose unique to each of us, became *The Enchanted Self*.

I developed a paradigm shift in my treatment, using my clients' memories to retrieve good times, happy times, and funny times and to focus on the functional aspects of their childhood rather than the dysfunctional. I began to teach clients how to recognize and itemize their talents and lost potential, how to view their lives as joyful journeys even with their many twists and turns, disappointments and complications.

I began to find that if we practice, we can recognize what brings us pleasure and joy, that it's not so hard to put that into words, and even to have more of it. The joy can come from a very small thing, as with a client who told me how elated she felt just taking a bath for half an hour with the door closed and a couple of candles lit, away from her children, her husband, and the television. There was a sense of returning to herself that was so special.

What I didn't realize by the time the first book was written was how I continued to grow spiritually and joyfully as I let in positive glimpses of life. I hadn't realized how many opportunities I would have to be charmed by others. But enchantment suddenly began streaming into my life from all directions. My clients were teaching *me* positive capacities, courage, and coping skills as fast as I could listen to them. Strangers were giving me lessons in wisdom and sharing their joy. Even people on television I would probably never meet were sharing good news. Forgotten fables and fairy tales, from my past and my present, were bringing joy into my life. So many random opportunities were giving me a sense of hope and a belief that the miraculous can happen.

Those responding to my book, *THE ENCHANTED SELF, A Positive Therapy*, to *THE ENCHANTED SELF Newsletter*, to the website, www.enchantedself.com, and to my presentations, were pouring forth their experiences, sharing their moments of enchantment, joy, and happiness. They wrote me e-mail, they sent their stories to the newsletter, and they became my guests on *THE ENCHANTED SELF* radio show and recounted positive events from their lives. It quickly became apparent that a new book would be emerging. *RECIPES FOR ENCHANTMENT* is the result.

There are three ingredients in any "recipe for enchantment." The first ingredient is a positive feeling within oneself – of optimism, hope, a sense of well being, purpose, determination, wholeness. You will see more nuances of these feelings in the book. The second major ingredient is a positive action, such as sharing, giving, loving, helping, befriending. The third major ingredient that is always necessary is your uniqueness, your perceptions of the world, reactions, interests, abilities, and passions. In essence, all three ingredients are parts of YOU. That is why I say that YOU are the secret ingredient – your positive energies combine with your unique history, your strengths and hidden potential to create *RECIPES FOR ENCHANTMENT.* Again and again you create magic by combining your positive feelings with positive action in your special way. Let me illustrate with two short episodes about real people.

Kay's happiest memories as a child were with a pencil and a sketchpad or with watercolors. Her life as an adult was very stressful and hectic. She had difficult teenagers and a marriage that perhaps many of you can identify with, one that left much to be desired. Her husband was often harsh and critical. One of her goals in treatment was to get back some of the joy she had experienced as a child.

Over the months she had practiced taking time for herself in order to do this, particularly to draw. Talking about her recent vacation in the Bahamas, she said, "Oh, it's filled with all the usual family bickering, but I'm so proud of myself. Every night as the sun set, I was able to get out my sketchpad and draw. I didn't allow my family to get in the way of this wonderful part of me that I've rediscovered. I love being able to own my own talent. Inside I feel an excitement growing as I take sketchpad in hand and pick a color, looking out at an image and recapturing it on paper. There's almost a tingling inside of me, and I know that I'm coming closer to my true essence. I share everything else in my life, but my talent belongs to me."

Here's another little story, about Tess. Tess was very artistic as a child. She had loved making doll clothes and using bits of fabric to make clothespin dolls. But as a young adult, she had a boyfriend who, although he seemed perfect for her at first, became very negative, putting her down and making her feel unhappy. They finally broke up. Rather than feeling depressed, Tess felt liberated. She started making clothing again, but this time for herself and her friends, not for dolls. "I was able to tune into my younger self," she told me. Eventually she found a wonderful guy and married, walking down the aisle in a beautiful gown she had designed. "I agree that people have to get more in touch with what was positive in their youth and then be true to those parts of themselves," she says. "It really worked for me."

Each of these women came to focus on what was right about herself rather than what was wrong. As each did, positive changes occurred. All the stories that follow are designed to teach you about the happy outcomes that are available to all of us when we focus on the positive rather than on the negative. They are also designed to help you begin to construct a more meaningful life by giving you the courage, insight, wisdom, and humor to take more positive actions every day.

No, we cannot prevent life from being challenging, difficult, at times overwhelming and even despairing. But we can bring into our lives the special ingredients that turn even the most trying times into moments in which the human spirit triumphs.

Each little story or glimpse that I share comes to you from my special collection of "recipes for enchantment." Like any good recipe box, this collection has grown over the years through many sources. There are clippings from all sorts of writings I have read, short accounts from things I saw on television, and wonderful stories that clients and friends have told me, or that other people have sent in to my newsletter.

When you eat something delicious, it feels good and it warms your heart as well as your stomach. A "recipe for enchantment" also feels good, provides nourishment, gives you a sense of well being and, hopefully, sets your mind, heart, and spirit in motion to create more enchantment.

Some of the words that can be ingredients in the recipes include giving, helping, trusting, forgiving, remembering, forgetting, loving, hoping, thanking and caring. I am encouraging you to focus on positive actions because that's what's required to create a sense of well being in one's life, or a shared sense of joyfulness and pleasure. This action may involve the simple step of thinking about someone in a positive light, or looking for the good in an event. Or it may be a more involved sequence of steps that requires brainstorming, problem solving, perhaps even learning a new way of living.

As you can see, actions taken in our lives can have both positive and negative consequences. Some words, such as "remembering," can be used both positively and negatively. You may reminisce about the worst times in your life, or the best times in your life. The focus will be different, the feeling aroused will be very different and the information taken from these memories will lead to different consequences. This is part of the tremendous responsibility and awesomeness of being human. Indeed we are capable of taking the best from a situation, whether it's in the past or present, or the worst, remembering what didn't work and allowing ourselves to feel discouraged, hopeless and fearful as a result.

However, your uniqueness remains priceless and is often stored in your memories. At the end of each story, you will find a learning opportunity. You can take the major ingredient in that particular story – sharing, caring, loving – and search your own memory bank for a unique experience in which you or someone else took a positive action. If you wish, you can write about that experience and in doing so, bring to life the "seasonings" that are uniquely yours – your background, your interests, your values, your potential. Often you can use the activity following each story as a jumping off point to stimulate personal growth or merely for yourself and pleasure.

Above all, let this book serve as a means for you to see your gifts through reflecting on these extraordinary, yet ordinary, people. Take the time to acknowledge what makes you special and let your courage to truly become your *ENCHANTED SELF* come through.

Let a sense of well-being permeate your life. Let joy become your rightful companion. Proudly live a life of purpose, unique to your style, your talents, abilities and potential. The stories I've included have been chosen intuitively by me as useful teaching stories. I believe their particular voices serve as mentors whose vibrational energies go out to you. They can help us create larger and larger circles of harmony and good will, circles where we live lives of meaning and experience joy while feeling to our very core our uniqueness and our personal capacities for inspiration.

My journey has led me to the following conclusions that I would like to share with you as you go on to read these stories:

- ❋ You are entitled to joy, pleasure and repeated states of well being.
- ❋ You're entitled to a life of meaning.
- ❋ You are unique and the world needs your special gift.
- ❋ The story of your life is your most precious gift and the most precious gift you can share with others. The stories of your life contain all the information you need to recognize your talents, interests, preferences, skills and potential. How you use your uniqueness in a positive fashion is your personal assignment.
- ❋ All the lessons you will ever need are being taught all the time around you – stay open to them.
- ❋ Never forget that you're also one of those loving teachers. View yourself in a positive way filled with light and always available to mentor someone to cheer her up, to share some wisdom whether you can see it in yourself or not. Rest assured that you are one of the messengers of enchantment.

A BLESSING
I am changed by you Forever
Let it be good!
Let my influence on you be life-enhancing and yours on mine
May we learn from each other, golden threads of selfhood and together may we make a life-enhancing tapestry
Let me always remember that the teacher is in the student
And, in awe, I see the beauty in all.

You have the opportunity to participate after reading each story or vignette in this book. My hope is that you will do so and then, like any good cook, pass back to the universe your very best "enchanted recipes." To do this, please send your stories to me at encself@aol.com so that *RECIPES FOR ENCHANTMENT* can continue with Volume II.

May this little book and the activities that follow inspire you.

BAKING

<u>Loaves of Love</u>

One beautiful Wednesday morning, I drove from my home in suburban New Jersey to Borough Park in Brooklyn, a densely populated Jewish neighborhood. Men in long beards, little boys with side curls, and women wearing long, dignified skirts and wigs filled the streets. On a street of small grocery stores and plain row houses with well-kept gardens, I found Toby's house. She stood at the top of a long staircase, and seemed delighted to see me – a warm, friendly woman without a hint of make-up. Her hair was covered with a kerchief and she wore a housedress that looked like a bathrobe, the kind my grandmother used to wear. She also looked five months pregnant. I later discovered that she had 10 children – the oldest, 22, was already married – but only one was currently at home, a little girl, about two and a half, who clung to her mommy's apron strings.

Toby ushered me into her clean, but by American standards, barren kitchen. There were no photographs or magnets on the refrigerator, no paintings or wallpaper of fruit and vegetables, no radio or television – in fact, no appliances at all. It was as simple a kitchen as I had ever seen. Yet the old stove was already warm. I immediately felt a sense of peacefulness, as if the whole apartment was radiating positive energy. The windows were open and even the Brooklyn air smelled

1

fresh. Children's voices and traffic noises wafted up from the street, combining to create a silence that somehow felt sacred.

Toby showed me a giant dishpan in which a batch of challah dough was already rising. She explained that we would need another batch and asked if I wanted to do this by hand or by electric mixer. I chose the hand method. I was craving to get my hands into the dough. Toby said that many women prefer using the mixer, which is easier. However, her radiant face indicated her implicit approval of my choice.

She then produced another giant dishpan and told me to combine five cups of sifted flour, a cup of oil, five egg yolks, and salt. The leavening yeast was left to rise in another dish. After a while, when she told me to mix the ingredients together, I plunged my hands into the redolent mass feeling as if I were a girl again, playing in a sandbox. I didn't stop mushing until Toby told me to roll the dough into a giant ball and place it on her countertop. It was time to knead.

What a transforming experience! I felt as if God's feminine side whispered in my ear, "You have a wonderful task to do and it involves working this dough to the point of pure pleasure." For half an hour I pressed, rolled, pushed, pulled, squeezed, turned and lifted the dough as hard as I could. Toby, an instinctive teacher, praised my kneading technique and the strength of my hands. I found myself talking about my grandmother and the homemade challah she made when I was young. My hands, it seemed, had been inherited from a long line of women empowered by a sacred undertaking.

When my hands and arms grew tired, Toby encouraged me to rest and have a snack – delicious marble cake, creamy cheesecake, and homemade coffee ice cream – all handmade from the egg whites left over from her challah baking.

After our snack, we returned to our baking. Toby produced a bowl in which the challah had already risen. That's when I realized that the batch I had fashioned would be presented to Toby's next student – a woman I didn't know but to whom I was giving something very special, just as a stranger had bequeathed her kneading bowl to me.

I cut my new dough into six pieces, which I then rolled into long, thin strips. Toby showed me how to braid them. I tried to follow her as she spoke: "Bring these two strips close together and then bring this one under them and then it goes up over the right." Or did she say left? "Then the other goes down, and then you start all over."

I loved braiding the dough. After all the loaves were shaped, we made some miniature loaves with the leftover dough. Everything went into the oven. Toby invited me to visit the neighborhood while the bread baked, so I shopped. The time flew by. When I returned, about an hour later, I found Toby walking down the steps from her house with big gray plastic garbage bags in her hand, filled with the fruit of our labor. She placed the bags in the passenger and back seats of my car. We hugged and kissed each other. She told me to come back any time for my next lesson.

The aroma filled the car.   I had enough challah to last at least a month. Toby climbed the stairs back to her family, and I began driving toward the Verrazano Bridge. It was rush hour, but I was calm. I felt as if I had accomplished something special, a feeling I hadn't had for years, perhaps not since I was a girl and learned how to skip or ride my bike. The scent of the challah and the memory of its baking replenished me. I had a restorative sense of a job well done.

How Can You Relate To This Story?

One of the core ingredients for a Recipe for Enchantment lies in the doing.

Sometimes this doing happens privately, even within one's own mind such as meditating. Sometimes it happens between people in ways that are refreshing such as playing together or visiting. There is also a concept of "doing good deeds." When we are doing in the service of others, often a host of positive emotions take place. The person doing the action can feel happy, uplifted, wanted, special, and certainly the person who is the recipient of the "doing" can feel joyful, contented, special, involved, loved.

✻ Think for a moment about when you have been "doing" in a way that either enriches your life or someone else's. Don't be shy – the hardest part of this may be giving yourself credit where credit is due. Have you helped someone out? Been there in a special way for a friend? Have you taken good care of yourself? Been your own best friend by an action you took – be it a pampering bath or finally divorcing an abusive spouse? Share some of your "doings" here.

✻ On the other hand have you felt good when someone gave to you by "doing"? Perhaps a teacher gave time and extra tutoring that made all the difference? Or a friend had a meal waiting when you got home from the hospital? Share what the person did and how it made you feel.

BELIEVING

Joey Figures it Out

Joey, the youngest child in his family, was almost universally adored. No one could resist a ten-year-old with red hair and freckles who always waved hello, sported an ear-to-ear grin, sent thank-you notes after receiving a present, and actually listened when adults talked to him. He had other talents as well. Not only was he the star batter on his local little league team, but he always impressed his teammates, their parents, and his coaches with his good nature and good sportsmanship. Joey was always ready to shake hands, and to offer a hand in need.

But one spring, with little league practice just three weeks away, Joey became sick with a headache and body pains that wouldn't quit. His concerned parents took him for tests that revealed the worst: Joey had cancer.

Though the hospitalizations were grueling, Joey survived the first ones with his good humor intact. But during his last stay, he became withdrawn and quiet, barely speaking a word to anyone. His nurses, doctors, parents and grandparents all became terribly concerned. Joey the fighter was gone. In his place was a boy they didn't know who seemed to be acquiescing to his disease.

One day, a middle-aged woman appeared in his hospital room and said, "Joey, I'm Mrs. Davis and I've been sent here by your school to work with you on your English. I'll be here three times a week for one hour. You have an awful lot of work to make up, so let's get started." Mrs. Davis worked with Joey on vocabulary and diagramming sentences, gave him some homework, and said she'd be back in two days.

Upon her return, the nurses caught up with her before she had a chance to enter Joey's room. They were amazed, they said, that after weeks of little or no progress, Joey had perked up and seemed like his old self. The nurses attributed the change to Mrs. Davis. She was flattered – but puzzled. She couldn't understand how diagramming sentences and memorizing vocabulary words could have changed Joey's attitude.

At the end of the session, after assigning Joey's homework, she asked how he was feeling.

"I'm feeling so much better, Mrs. Davis. I really think I'm going to get well. You'll see, I'll be playing baseball before the season is even finished."

"That's wonderful," Mrs. Davis said. "What makes you so sure you'll be playing?"

"Well," Joey said, "my school would never have sent you here to work with me on verbs and vocabulary if I wasn't going to make it. They must think I'm going to get better or they wouldn't waste all this money. So you know what? I'm going back to school, and to baseball practice, as soon as I can."

How Can You Relate To This Story?

So often our attitude and perception of events make a huge difference not only in the ways we interpret our lives but in the strength and endurance we bring to our lives so that we can go on living. And often our attitudes and perceptions are derived from how we first react to a situation. This was certainly the case for Joey. What Mrs. Davis' appearance meant to him was that the school system counted on his getting well. Their time together indicated to Joey that he was worth the school's financial investment in his future.

✤ Can you remember an occasion when your reaction to a situation led to positive action?

I remember a beautiful example in my life. When I was in third grade, I could hardly read because I had undiagnosed dyslexia. Frustrated - unable to keep up with even the lowest reading group - I felt a sense of dread every time the teacher asked us to take out our reading books. One day Mrs. Johnson called me up to her desk and she said, "Barbara, I can see you're having a lot of trouble reading, and I have a suggestion. You're a smart little girl with a good memory. Why don't you stop trying to sound out words and instead simply memorize them? Soon you'll know hundreds and then thousands of words by sight and by the time you finish third grade, you will be a very good reader - I promise you."

9

Her words inspired me, giving me the courage and confidence I needed to learn to read. Actually, I'd been trying her approach in secret. But her permission, combined with my eagerness to please her, gave me a burst of energy. By the end of third grade, I had memorized so many sight words that I won the prize for having read the most library books.

* I hope you can remember a time when you were similarly inspired and found the courage to change your behavior. It may take a little while to think of an episode in your life, as often we tend to dismiss the encouraging words others give us.

Come back to this page anytime if nothing comes to you now.

On the other hand...

* Can you think of something positive you could say to anyone in your life right now?

It's possible that your encouragement might make a huge difference in that person's life. Maybe there's something you could do for someone, the way Mrs. Davis came to the hospital to tutor Joey. Over the next few weeks, think about your potential to create positive change in someone else's life – and consider doing it.

BELONGING

When Saturday was Really Saturday
Bernice Becker

"Bernice, are you almost ready? We're leaving for Grandma and Grandpa's soon."

"Yes, Mom, I'm almost finished brushing my hair." I wanted my hair to shine the way Grandma Sara's lustrous dark hair did. I was nine years old, and dressed in my best Saturday outfit - a sapphire blue blouse and a plaid shirt that blended with the top. I wore my black patent Mary Janes, which made me feel special.

My parents, two brothers - Arnold and Howard - and I were invited for a 12:30 Shabbat dinner. Grandma's cooking was better than anyone else's, even my Mom's. Perhaps we'd have a stuffed capon or a pot roast with little roasted potatoes.

Grandma and Grandpa lived with three unmarried sons, one of whom, Herbie, was adopted, and one daughter, Aunt Ethel. Orphaned at age two during a terrible flu epidemic, Herbie had been raised by the Watchmakers who lavished attention and love on him. The family had a loyal housekeeper who did the cleaning. But Grandma shouldered the enormous cooking and baking chores for the large family. My grandfather was Orthodox and he wouldn't eat out except where kosher food was served. My Aunt Ethel excelled in the desserts.

As we walked the several short blocks to Ruthven Street, we exchanged greetings with the people we knew. Folks were strolling along Elm Hill Avenue where the streets were lined with wonderful, stately elm trees in full bloom on this spring day. The mingled fragrances of honeysuckles and lilacs perfumed the air. When I took a deep breath it was like a cool sweet drink. I felt connected to my neighborhood and enjoyed the comforting sense of belonging.

Before we reached our destination our mother cautioned us, "Be polite and watch your manners."

"It's gross when your mouth is full and you're talking," Arnold said.

Howard added, "You shouldn't stuff your mouth anyway. You could choke."

We reached Ruthven Street and walked up one flight to the spacious nine-room apartment where our grandparents were waiting for us. As the baby of the family, I got extra hugs. I soon detected the mouth-watering aroma of potato kugel – a good welcome.

In the living room, we were served fresh kichel bread with chopped chicken livers – well worth their weight in gold and cholesterol. "No one can make kichel and chopped liver like you," my mother told her mother. "It's the absolute best."

The chairs in the gracious dining room were upholstered in burgundy and gold damask, which matched the drapes. The sparkling chandelier cast its light on the crystal goblets, gleaming silver candlesticks and fine china. Grandma had crocheted the champagne lace tablecloth herself. When I saw the dish with jumbo green olives on the table, I said, "Oh, you remember how I love those." Then Grandpa, who was short but handsome in his velvet smoking jacket and yarmulke, made a prayer over the golden brown braided challah from which we each took a piece before dinner was served.

First we ate fresh fruit cup with sherbet, which was followed by tender, lean brisket of beef au jus, with candied carrots, stuffed mushrooms and wonderful kugel. The men talked about prize fighting and the famous champion of the era, Jack Dempsey. The women discussed recipes and the current stage shows in downtown Boston.

Encouraged to participate in the conversation, I related the story of my neighbor, Tootsie Freedman, who accidentally got a cherry pit stuck up her nose. The pit moved up and down with her breathing, but wouldn't come out. Her frantic mother, Tootsie, and I drove to the Children's Hospital, where the offending object was removed. What a newsworthy story, I thought!

After a foot-high lemon meringue pie and hot tea with little fruit-flavored sugar cubes, our delicious meal was over. Everyone made the usual comments about the fabulous food. Heaven only knows how many pounds we had gained that day.

All the children went to play in Herbie's bedroom; all his great books, games and puzzles were a treat for us. None of us had such a large stock of material goodies. After we had played for a couple of hours, our parents told us that it was time to go home. I didn't want to leave, but Grandma reminded me that I'd be visiting during the week, after school.

At the front door, my affectionate, generous Grandpa Isaac placed a dollar bill in my hand. "For you, Shayna," he said. My brothers received their share also. We were fortunate to have him for one more year. Walking home satisfied and well fed, I sensed our silent consensus that we had spent another memorable Saturday seated around the bountiful table "breaking bread together."

This was one of the times in my life when I could sense my ENCHANTED SELF emerging. I had such positive feelings when I was surrounded by my loving family. Occasions such as these were unforgettable, and I cherish the memories of when Saturday was really Saturday.

Food has always been important in my life. Sometimes I feel guilty because I think about and enjoy food so much, but then I realize that "breaking bread" with family and friends has always been a way of life for me. So many wonderful memories are associated with the holiday celebrations, or with Saturday afternoons, sitting around the table feeling connected to the people I care about and who care about me.

Thankfully, I am pretty well in control about what I eat and I do watch my weight. Besides, I have many interests other than eating.

Well, I must stop writing now. My lunch is ready and it smells so inviting….

How Can You Relate To This Story?

This is such a great story because it helps us acknowledge that belonging to a loving family soothes and refreshes us much the way the aromas from a savory meal whets and then satisfies our appetite. Not everyone has had a chance to feel as special as Bernice felt when, as a child, she trusted that her story about Tootsie Freedman would be welcome and appreciated by the other adults. But I hope that you have shared a good meal with friends or family during which you felt special or acknowledged, or during which the food itself was an acknowledgment of the special regard in which the others held you.

* *Can you remember a special meal? Replenish yourself by going back in time to that wonderful meal, where everything was so enjoyable – the food as well as the company! Take a few minutes and let the memory come back to you: the smells, the tastes, the atmosphere of the room, the weather, what you wore, what was happening at that time in your life. Can you think of one word to describe the most special quality about that occasion? Perhaps words like "belonging," "replenishing," "sharing" or "connecting" come to mind.*

✳ *Now brainstorm three ways that you could get close to that quality again. For example, if I were Mrs. Becker, I might decide that the most important quality was "sharing." If so, I might invite some dear friends to my home and serve them some of the wonderful foods from my childhood memories. Or if I decide that I want to emphasize belonging, I might make an effort to get together with family members who are still around. In this case, the food might be secondary, taking a back seat to the importance of being with them again.*

CARING

Doggy Day Care

Watching CBS this morning, I saw a wonderful story that touched my heart. It was about an extraordinary, long overdue innovation – day care for dogs! Located in Manhattan (where else!), the center watches over dogs while their owners go off to work.

I saw a snippet of film about what happens during morning drop-off time. One by one, pet owners come in with their pets on their way to work, and say goodbye. In the center, the dogs can hardly contain their happiness: they leap up and lick their day-care friends. Together, dogs and caregivers enter a big room that resembles a gym with a beautiful wood floor. Some dogs want to play, some lounge, and some work out – on specialized treadmills and other sports equipment.

Most remarkable of all, the dogs' owners can watch their pets. The center contains concealed video cameras that transmit images over the internet. With this arrangement, the dogs don't know they're being watched so they are not distracted, but their owners can make sure that their pets are happily enjoying themselves. (I have a feeling that many children's day care centers will want to install video cameras as well so that anxious parents can assure themselves that their children are doing fine, just as the dog owners can.)

At the end of the day, owners retrieve their happy pets before going home. Rather than having to mark time in an empty apartment, the pets have had a full day of companionship and kinship.

This program touched my heart for several reasons. First, it fills a real need. In our lonely society, with so many people living separate lives, we turn to pets for friendship and love. Yet when we go off to work, we make our poor pets stay by themselves to wander the house, chew slippers, jump on furniture, stare woefully out of windows. It's so much more sensible to bring our dogs to a day care facility where they can receive loving care and attention. Yes, animals need an emotional network as much as we do!

It's also an enchanting story because the person who created Doggy Day Care did something positive in the world by identifying a need and filling it. Clearly, the idea is a good one since so many people are using the facility. In this story, everyone ends up feeling good: the owners, who are making a good living from the center; the pet owners, who know they are doing right by their animals; and the pets themselves. There's nothing wrong with a Recipe for Enchantment that addresses God's other creatures.

How Can You Relate To This Story?

This is a wonderful story that you can refer to when you have the urge to make the world a better place. Try to brainstorm some ideas now. Let your imagination run wild. You are the CEO of this project, and your budget is limitless.

So often, a small, overdue correction or invention makes a huge difference. A slight turn, shift in perspective, or new interpretation can cause huge changes in the course of our lives and of the world. For example, think about the First Temple built in Jerusalem, which I was privileged to visit a few years ago. In structure, it resembled all the temples that had been built before it.

The worship service there was also similar to those in other temples – priests sacrificed animals and used purified water. But there was one difference that ended up changing the future of mankind: before the construction of the First Temple, people prayed to many gods. But when people came to worship at the Temple in Jerusalem, they prayed to one God. From that point forward, history was changed forever.

We're all capable of assessing the world in which we live and intuitively grasping which small corrections may have an enormous impact. I've noticed several such corrections in the past few years – billboards suggest that we indulge in random acts of kindness; organizations adopt stretches of highway to keep litter-free; people band together to create community gardens in public spaces in our cities and towns; tutors visit students and shut-ins at home to instruct them in various subjects such as computer science.

Here's another example: job-sharing, which my father, who devoted his career to education, advocated. In this way, two people, whether teachers or administrators, split one position between them, allowing each person more time to conduct the rest of his or her life. According to this model, one plus one equals more than two since each person will work more than fifty percent of the time, and will be more than half invested in the job. In addition, two people will be able to be active members of the professional world for the cost of one paycheck. Best of all, the beneficiaries – in this case, the children – will benefit from more help and expertise than they've paid for.

* Now take some time to brainstorm some positive corrections that you've come up with. Remember, you're in complete charge and money is no object. Have fun changing some of the ways we construct our daily lives.

Return to what you've written here once in a while and see if any of your ideas urge you into action. If so, you may be on the road to making an extraordinary, long overdue innovation. Good luck!

COMPLETING

<u>Mr. Diamond's Last Trip through Elizabeth</u>

When Mr. Diamond recently passed away, everyone in his neighborhood was bereft. They knew him not only as the local butcher, but as a warm, generous man to whom many had turned over the years for help and advice. Even before his funeral, stories of his kindness began to circulate. "Remember the packages of meat he used to leave at your front door? If you ordered four lamb chops, you'd open it to find three pounds of ground beef and some bones for a cholent stew as well – and a bill for only the four chops."

People also remembered how thoughtful he was about lending money, never asking any questions. Over the years, his wife and neighbors had encouraged him to invest some of his savings. But Mr. Diamond always said, "Who knows if these monetary investments will ever pay off? What I do for my friends – that's my investment in the future."

The day of his funeral dawned gloomy and gray. Because Mr. Diamond was going to be buried in Israel, there was a long motorcade procession to the airport. Police escorts from surrounding towns led the cortege along the most direct route. But at one point the procession was diverted through the downtown streets of Elizabeth, New Jersey. No one knew why. Did the police officers make a mistake? Almost a half-hour elapsed before the procession was re-routed onto a major road.

Mr. Diamond's son turned to his mother and said, "Why do you think we drove through Elizabeth? Did Daddy ever have a connection there?" It was as if this boy had great faith and knew that nothing happens by chance.

"As a matter of fact," Mrs. Diamond began, "Daddy did have a connection in Elizabeth. Years ago, he did business with a slaughterhouse there, which he soon realized was passing off non-kosher meat as kosher. For example, they claimed to have 20 kosher carcasses on hand and yet 25 kosher tongues. Impossible! After he passed this information on to the authorities, the slaughterhouse was quickly closed down."

"Everyone knew that the slaughterhouse was owned by the Mafia," Mrs. Diamond continued. "Friends encouraged your father never to set foot in Elizabeth again. And he never did – until today."

Was it an "accident" that the police officer leading the funeral cortege lost his way? Perhaps Mr. Diamond in some way engineered the mistake, realizing that now that he was untouchable, he could safely return to the town of Elizabeth one more time in order to complete the circle of his life.

How Can You Relate To This Story?

This story is about divine justice – about people finding recognition, having the last word, or righting a

25

wrong that occurred many years ago. Let me explain with an example from my own life. Years ago, Boston University had to cancel its graduation ceremonies due to student rioting. It happened to be the year I was to receive my Doctorate in Education, a degree I'd worked long and hard to attain. Instead of the formal ceremony to which I'd been looking forward, I had to content myself with a celebratory dinner with my family.

Twenty-five years later, I received an invitation from the University to attend graduation ceremonies. My first reaction was to decline. After all, I technically had my degree. Also, the thought of attending the ceremony seemed particularly out of synch with my stage of life: graduating was for young adults, and here I was, in my middle years. Not only that, but I'd have to drive to Boston, meet up with people I hadn't seen in many years, and put on a cap and gown which would probably make me feel foolish. But because my parents were eager to see me graduate – the whole process felt incomplete to them as well as to me – and my husband and son agreed to accompany me, I agreed to attend.

As it turned out, the ceremony was thrilling, and I was delighted to reconnect with so many old friends. So what if I was older? I gained a sense of completion, and allowed myself to enjoy the feeling of being honored. In truth, I was probably more relaxed and appreciative of the festivities than I would have been 25 years earlier.

From this very belated graduation ceremony I learned that sometimes we have to seize important opportunities. Even those that seem "out of synch" with our present-day lives may have special relevance to us, and help us to complete our life journeys.

* ❋ *Have you ever completed something left incomplete in your life?*

* ❋ *Have you known someone who was able to complete such an act?*

* ❋ *Perhaps there's something in your life that you still need to complete. And perhaps you'll need to take some action in order to accomplish this. Maybe you have to get together with someone whom you knew years ago even though this may entail traveling to visit that person; perhaps you need to finally finish an abandoned project. Use this opportunity to think about unfinished business in your life and jot down notes about how you can begin. Remember, most of us don't need to wait for our funeral cortege to execute unfinished business.*

CONNECTING

Sally's Family Ties

The Greene family - Sally, her husband Bob, and their twelve-year-old daughter Sara - had outgrown their house. The snug, two-bedroom Cape Cod into which they'd moved soon after Sara's birth, had been a wonderful home for all those years. But now, with Sara on the brink of adolescence, it was proving much too small. After months of discussion and probing questions - should they move? build an extension? - they decided to gut the house and build a new one on the same site. They pored over plans for the new house, hired an architect and a contractor, and were told that the project would take about five months. In the interim, they decided to rent a tiny apartment in town. Sally dreaded the idea. It seemed so ironic - here they were, trying to expand their living quarters, and ending up with even less space than they were used to. Unfortunately, there was no other solution. But Sally was in for a surprise. For after only a week of living in the new apartment, she realized that this move was a godsend. None of her worries had materialized. There were no fights over privacy, no harsh words, no tense moods. Quite the opposite! Living in the cramped apartment, her family was drawn closer together than they'd been in years.

In their old house, for example, there were two TVs, one in each bedroom. The apartment had room for only one which they put it in the living room. As a result, they tended to watch television together. But best of all, they watched less TV.

Sally noticed other changes. In their old house, Sara tended to take her time in the downstairs bathroom she had to herself. With only one bathroom in the apartment for all three of them to share, Sara showed surprising thoughtfulness and courtesy. She neither hogged the mirror nor spent too much time in the shower.

Bob was also changing. In their old house, he'd get up immediately after dinner and retreat to the living room to read the newspaper. Now, he lingered at the kitchen table, taking time to talk to her and to Sara. He began to ask about the details of their lives in ways he never had, and showed interest in all their activities. The more he knew, the more he wanted to know. And because he better understood his wife and daughter, he was less irritable around the house. In fact, everyone was kinder to each other.

The small, temporary space fostered a welcome sense of interconnectedness and belonging. Sally sometimes found herself wishing that they wouldn't have to leave. But her deepest wish was that her family could preserve their newfound closeness and take it with them to their new house. Who would have thought that their newfound closeness would become their most precious possession!

How Can You Relate To This Story?

A few years ago, I became friends with the Rosens, an orthodox Jewish family. As was typical, they had a large family - eight children - and lived in a modest home with no television. Yet despite their close quarters, they led very private lives sanctified by prayer. Rachel and her husband treated each other and their children with respect. The older children helped younger ones. I remember in particular one Shabbos afternoon when even though fourteen children were playing at one end of the living room, I was actually able to have a conversation with four other women - in the same room! Yes, something positive was going on in that family. Thanks to mutual respect, the family had developed in such a way that everyone had time and space. They were able to get to know each other, relax, take a nap, talk to friends - all within a small, shared space.

❋ Have you ever known a family like the Rosens? Or did you know a family in which the members felt isolated from each other? Do you feel isolated? What helps you to feel more a part of a family or closer to others? Jot down notes that respond to any of the above questions here.

✸ Tell a story about a time in your life when everyone shared and felt connected - for example, at a family reunion, or the time the lights went out.

DANCING

Dancing the Sardana
Claire Wintram

Forty years ago, when I was eight, I was on holiday with my parents and four-year-old sister in northern Spain. To me, an Anglo-Jewish child from an English Midlands village with only loose connections to the local urban Jewish community, the country seemed full of magic.

Everything entranced me: eating on the patio of the restaurant under the stars, watching women carrying live chickens and guinea fowl in baskets to market, and savoring the tiny delicious pastries and pastel-colored ice cream with unimaginable subtle flavors. I remember the intensity of light reflected in the rock pools on the beach, the sights and sounds of the local fairground where we made ourselves sick on the swing boats, the huge billboards rising up out of the middle of maize fields, and the sight of donkeys pulling farm carts wearing hats with holes for their ears. In retrospect, this holiday, with its countless vibrant images, is overflowing with ENCHANTED MOMENTS.

But the most wonderful ENCHANTED MOMENT happened one night. I'd already gone to sleep in my white nightdress spangled with tiny, deep blue stars. Sometime during the middle of the night, my father woke me up and told me to put clothes on over my nightdress. Leaving my sleeping sister and mother behind, we went downstairs, crossed the hotel lobby, and stepped into the moonlit square.

A crowd of people was dancing the Sardana, an ancient, graceful dance. Turning round and round in circles, arms linked across shoulders, they looked both happy and stately.

It was wondrous and exciting to see people dancing in the street, something I'd never before witnessed. Even though I was only a spectator of this joyful scene, I felt privileged. As I stood there, holding my father's hand, bewitched by the sight, one of the waiters from our hotel approached us, bowed solemnly, and invited me to join the dance with him. Astonished and delighted, I agreed.

I was filled with anxious pleasure as I joined the circle of celebration. I didn't know the steps, but it didn't matter. People were friendly and welcoming, and we spoke to each other beyond language. I felt honored, even in my youthfulness – a feeling I hadn't experienced in England. I danced for I don't know how long.

The images of that magical night with its ENCHANTED MOMENT have stayed with me all these years. But I am sure that its influence goes much deeper than conscious memory. For example, though I have always loved watching flamenco and taking part in Spanish and Latin American dances, I have only recently begun to discover the connections between gypsy and Jewish dancing and flamenco. This awareness has helped me understand my responses to the vibrant,

34

sensuous movements so characteristic of Spanish music. Despite my obvious Ashkenazi heritage, I am sure that I have Sephardic blood in my veins - I can feel its presence in my soul.

I am convinced that the ENCHANTED MOMENT I experienced as a child in Spain forty years ago recurs for me now when I hear certain dance music today, as an adult woman. The Sardana has surely had a significant and lasting impact on my life.

How Can You Relate To This Story?

Think about Claire as a young child dancing in the moonlight, bewitched by the grace, charm and responsiveness of the dancers. It's a magical scene. How wonderfully proud of herself she must have felt - and so alive. It's a wonderful, strengthening feeling to experience yourself as totally accepted by those around you, and in the center of an intense activity.

I remember an event that was much more private but left me feeling strong, appealing and special. When I was 11, my parents and I were vacationing in Provincetown, Massachusetts. I begged them to let me take an airplane ride over the town - and finally they agreed. Never in my wildest imagination could I have understood their courage in letting me go. Neither of them had ever flown at all - and I'd be sitting in one of the single-engine plane's two seats, right behind the pilot!

I remember my parents waving to me as the plane soared higher and higher. Up, up, up we went until all the houses seemed tinier than the tiniest dollhouses. The sky was blue with fluffy clouds and I felt literally on top of the world. The handsome pilot was kind and gracious to me. At some moment, I must have indicated that I was feeling somewhat anxious because I remember him saying to me, "If you wish, you can hold my hand for a while." There I was, up in the sky, having achieved something no one else in my family had, and holding the hand of Prince Charming to boot!

All too quickly the ride was over. I could sense my parents' delight and relief in their smiles and hugs. For me, this was a moment of courage and independence. I remember feeling valued – not only by my parents who loved me without question, but also by a total stranger.

Let your mind drift back to various times in your life, and poke around until you remember a time when you experienced a moment of wonderment, connection, or courage. Maybe it was a time when you finally got your way, or when certain people included you in a special activity. Your experience may be as different from Claire's as mine was. If you're having trouble remembering such a time, here are some key words to help you get started: feeling accepted; feeling powerful; a moment of courage; total pleasure; a heightened moment; victory; a euphoric moment.

❀ *Now write your memories here.*

DISCOVERING

<u>The Mysterious Rabbi</u>

Once long ago, in central Europe, there was a Jewish boy, Joseph, who went off to live in a Yeshiva to study. His days were filled with prayer and learning. He particularly enjoyed his time studying with his favorite Rabbi. Oftentimes when he was daydreaming he would think that he wished he knew more about this Rabbi. "What did he do with his time when he wasn't with the boys?" he would muse. Every day the youngster had a study hall in an upstairs room of the big old building that served as the Yeshiva. He would gaze out of the window daydreaming. Gradually he noticed that his Rabbi, the very one he wished he knew about, walked away from this building and left the premises at exactly the same time every day. He could see him going off into the distance and then returning thirty or forty minutes later. He left the premises rain or shine regardless of how cold it was. Joseph became fascinated. Where did the Rabbi have to go at exactly the same time every day? He certainly didn't have time to get back and forth to his home and to have a meal with his family. Joseph tortured himself. After all, it was really none of his business but then again he so admired and respected his Rabbi. Didn't he deserve to know more about his life?

One day his ruminations got the best of him and he snuck out of the study hall waiting for the Rabbi to leave the campus. Sure enough at exactly three ten, the Rabbi left. There was Joseph, following him from well behind. The Rabbi went up one hill and then down a hill and through a neighborhood. Finally he stopped and stood at the bottom of the busy street on the curb. The Rabbi just stood as if he had stopped dead in his tracks. He appeared to be waiting. Joseph was perplexed. What was going to happen now? The moments began to tick by. Nothing was going on here except push carts and horses and buggies were going up and down this busy business street. Suddenly a peddler pushing a very large heavy cart appeared down the end of the street. Joseph noticed the Rabbi insistently waving until the two of them made eye contact and the peddler came nearer to him. As the peddler came very near with his heavy cart, he moved from the center towards the left of his cart so that his hands were now on the left side pushing. He had left space at the right and to Joseph's amazement, what happened next was something of which Joseph never would have dreamed. The Rabbi moved in effortlessly next to the peddler, and put his hands on the right hand side of the bar. Together, with great effort exuded by both of them, they pushed the peddler's cart up the steep hill. Then at the top of the hill, just as effortlessly, the Rabbi moved away from the cart, simply waving goodbye. The peddler again moved into the middle to balance his cart and the Rabbi came down the hill. The Rabbi's face was flushed as he came back towards campus. He wiped his forehead with a handkerchief where the perspiration was still pouring off of him. Joseph thought as he

40

watched him that he had the glow of a person who has been helpful. A couple of minutes later he was back in the building preparing for his next class.

Joseph thought to himself, "So that's what the Rabbi does with his forty five minutes off campus everyday. He goes and waits for a peddler, an ordinary man, a stranger who has a heavy burden and he helps that man up the hill." Joseph was amazed and even more in awe of his Rabbi.

This story adapted from the Mussar movement in Jewish history is a beautiful example of an earth angel. It always amazes me how good I can suddenly feel when I've been truly helpful. But perhaps I have an even more heightened sense of joy if I get a chance to be helpful in a capacity that is not part of my normal repertoire. That's what this Rabbi was doing. A very learned scholar, he was now offering his arms and his brute strength in a simple way, repetitively every day to a stranger.

How Can You Relate To This Story?

I can remember one time when I suddenly stretched myself to help a stranger. In this case, it was a poodle dog. I was walking and saw a dog trembling with a tattered bandage, half off. This bandage appeared to have been around his abdomen. I myself have never owned a dog and am not particularly comfortable around them. My love is cats. But I found myself scooping up this poodle who was so frightened and feeling his relief as he settled into my arms. It was a simple step to walk the few blocks with him to a veterinarian's office that I knew was located down the street. I sat waiting with the dog, to give him over to the veterinarian and found myself filled with a sense of purpose and sudden love for this little creature. It was a shocking sense of connection that I had never expected to experience. Not only was I feeling good about having helped this little dog, but I actually began to hope that I might get a chance to adopt him if no one else came forth.

The good news was that his owner indeed had not abandoned him and soon came looking for him at the veterinarian's. So he was safe and cared for again. The bad news was that I had to settle for my positive feelings of helping and going out of my way to stretch myself with new behaviors rather than suddenly becoming this dog's new parent.

* Can you think of a time when you had a chance to be helpful, particularly a time when you were helpful in a way that wasn't tied to your normal roles or your profession? Tell the story here.

✻ If you can't think of a time, let your heart begin to be open to the universe, indicating that you are willing to help out. I am certain that the divine will pick up on your energies and let you be an earth angel quicker than you can possibly imagine. If that happens, come back later and capture the episode in words on this page.

FINDING

<u>There By the Grace of God</u>

Phyllis, a young retired woman, lives and travels with her husband in a mobile home. They enjoy our beautiful country, and manage to stay in touch thanks to a cellular phone and constant access to e-mail.

Last year, camping in a national park, Phyllis noticed a cat sleeping on their picnic table. Presuming it was a hungry stray, she left some scraps on the table. After a while, she noticed that the cat hadn't touched the food, which seemed odd. Usually stray animals are hungry for any morsel. Curious, she started to walk toward the cat, talking softly all the while. But then she stopped dead in her tracks. Part of the cat's face had literally been ripped off. No wonder she couldn't eat – her jaw was injured.

Phyllis was upset beyond words. She wanted to bring the cat to the local veterinarian. However, it was the day before July Fourth, and her husband was leery – he worried that the cat had a disease. Though he finally agreed to accompany Phyllis to find a vet and a cat carrier, he assured her that by the time they returned the cat would be gone.

He was right.

Phyllis felt terrible. She and her husband were supposed to leave the next day, but she realized that she couldn't leave without knowing what had happened to that poor, injured cat, unable to eat, hiding somewhere in the woods. Her husband said, "Don't be ridiculous. If the cat's gone, she's gone. She knows instinctively how to take care of herself and she's not gonna come back." Needless to say their Fourth of July was filled with friction and frustration.

But this time it was Phyllis who was right. The next morning, the cat wandered back. Phyllis was ready. Wearing thick gloves, she put the cat in the carrier she'd borrowed, and called Annie, a woman she'd learned of who lived nearby and who saved animals.

When they met, Phyllis gave Annie the carrier with the poor cat huddled in a corner. Annie promised to keep Phyllis informed. Sure enough, she called a few days later to say that the cat needed several operations, and that some young veterinarians had volunteered their services.

Though the operations were successful, the cat would have to eat by a tube for months. Because the veterinarians were not prepared to keep the cat during the long months of recovery, Annie adopted the cat, whom she named Grace, as in "There but for the Grace of God."

As Phyllis traveled around the country, she called Annie for Grace's medical updates. Grace was making good progress - she could lick her blended food, though she was as yet still unable to chew.

To Phyllis, Annie's name should have been Grace as well. For Annie not only took in stray cats, but also cared for ten other animals, including an abandoned donkey. In time, the donkey seemed lonely, so Annie found a mate. And wouldn't you know it – now Annie has a baby donkey to care for as well.

How Can You Relate To This Story?

This is a wonderful, true story about two insistent women, each dedicated to caring about life and not abandoning those in need. To all the Phyllises and Annies in this world, I want to say, "Thank you." You keep us on earth connected to the Divine.

Do you know someone or have heard of someone who is a wonderful doer? Perhaps she is someone who just quietly goes about her business helping others or protecting the environment, or being there when a child needs some extra tutoring or an ill person needs a visit. This is a good opportunity to take some time to write about that person. If you are writing about someone who is alive, you might think about sending her a thank-you note or mentioning to him that you appreciate what he's doing.

* Maybe that person is you. If so, write about what you do for those in your life. Pat yourself on the back and reward yourself with an extra treat. Maybe you want to buy yourself a gift, take a day off, indulge in a massage – or simply give yourself a secret hug.

GIVING

The Universe Comes through for Judy

Judy was on a real high today. She told me that a few months ago, her husband, Donald, had lost about $720. He had given the money to a salesman in a furniture store as a deposit on a beautiful bedroom set. The salesman turned out to be a crook: he kept the money for himself. Donald couldn't find his sales slip, and without it, the owner of the store wouldn't make up the loss. So he was out the money, and he and Judy were out the bedroom set.

They were terribly distressed. Judy's mother suggested they go to a second-hand furniture store such as the Salvation Army, where they might find a used brass bed or something else of decent quality. At the time, they were sleeping in an empty bedroom on a very worn mattress on the floor.

One day, as Judy and Donald were leaving her mother's apartment, they noticed a beautiful brass bed in the gutter. It appeared to be totally new, and they were stunned. Gradually, as they examined it more closely, they saw that the bed was slightly worn, although it still looked good. Next to it sat a mattress and box springs, both apparently in excellent condition. All three items were clearly being thrown out.

With growing excitement, Judy and her husband discussed how to hoist the bed. They carried it upstairs, cleaned off the mattress, put the bed together – and, low and behold, they had the most exquisite brass bed! To top if off, while Judy was examining the mattress and box springs, she noticed tags indicating that the two pieces had cost a total of about $720 retail. Later that week, Donald found a lovely old table in another gutter, and he fixed it up and used it as a nightstand. Judy had been given some money for her birthday, and she used it to complete the ensemble by buying a quilt, a bedspread, and a few lovely throw pillows. She was truly ecstatic – the universe had indeed come through.

❋ *Has the universe ever paid you back in full in a positive way? Tell the story.*

❋ *If not, what are three wishes you would like the universe to fulfill for you?*

GRIEVING

Memories, Grieving and Resolution
Bernadette Hoyer

I didn't cry when my father died nearly two years ago. In fact, I felt nothing – neither the intense anger and hatred that my sisters had toward him, nor the devoted, undying love that my mother professed (how I envied her for being able to feel that much unquestioning love for a person).

Never one to dwell on depressing thoughts, I'd always been able to talk or cry when I felt sad, until I felt cleansed. But with my father, I couldn't express how I was feeling. All I felt at the time was a sense of relief. I hoped that with his passing, our lives would turn to some type of "normality." I was eager to get on with it, but my surprising emotional paralysis concerned me.

My father touched my life in ways that I could never forget. He nurtured my strong will. He taught me to protect myself from unkind, greedy people. Determination, will and shrewdness – that's what he told me I would need to be a success in business. To teach me right from wrong, he shared his childhood stories with me. But he never allowed me to experiment on my own, to learn from my own hard knocks. As a result, I grew to adulthood not knowing how to take care of myself. I knew what I was supposed to do, but not how to do it.

This caused me a great deal of pain and loss. Whenever I would ask him for a sympathetic ear or help, he would say, "You made your bed, now you lie in it. I had nobody to help me!" This comment was so hurtful to hear. Eventually, the closeness I'd always felt with my father started to fade until, at his death, only numbness remained.

From time to time, I would search my heart and mind, trying to find the feeling that was sorely missing. I knew that I needed to grieve for him, but grief wouldn't come. Finally, I decided to get on with life. And so I did – until my mother died this past March. At her death I was able to cry, as I knew I would. Flooded by pain and sorrow, I smiled at the memories of her that I cherished. We had shared so many good times. Mourning for her, I kept searching for the link that would somehow release the flood of tears I knew I had stored up for my father. Nothing. The grief for my mother, however, took a long time to dissipate. Only months later could I speak about her without choking up. I continued on in my life as I knew I must.

Then, this morning, a memory flashed across my mind's viewing screen. I was tapping into my "ENCHANTED SELF" as I often do. I saw myself as a child playing with my dog Blackie in our yard. I was having so much fun with him! He was jumping hoops through my encircled arms, one of the many tricks he knew. I never questioned how he knew them or how he had come to be my dog. I only knew that Blackie and I loved each other and were very happy.

But this particular day, a man and woman walked by and asked me how Blackie knew those tricks. I told them I didn't know. They looked at each other a moment, and for some reason I started to feel afraid. "That's our dog," the man said.

Protectively, I grabbed Blackie and said, "No, he's my dog!" They asked how long I had had Blackie, and how old he was, and what his name was. I didn't know. Growing more and more frightened, I said, "I'm going to get my Daddy." Taking Blackie with me, I ran into the house for my father. I told him what happened, and begged him to tell these horrible people to go away.

He went outside. I watched from the front window. After an agonizingly long time, they left. When he came in, he told me that it was all taken care of. Relieved, I thanked him, hugged Blackie, and went on with my life.

When Blackie disappeared a short time later, it happened so quietly that I barely even noticed. I knew the ways of animals; sometimes they stayed and sometimes they strayed because they were "called" and they had to go. No one told me this. I just knew that deep inside an animal's heart was wild. I accepted this without question. In fact, I was glad. I knew in my heart that Blackie was all right and that someone else was having the opportunity to play with him and love him.

There I sat this morning, drinking my tea and remembering this story, and suddenly I was sobbing.

Tears for my father! I'd known for a long time that he'd made a deal with that couple to let me keep Blackie for a short time longer so that I wouldn't feel the pain of having the dog so abruptly torn from me, Though I'd replayed this memory many times, it had never before had this impact on me, and I knew it was time to grieve for my father.

By dealing with Blackie so sensitively, my father performed a great act of love. He knew how devastated my sisters and I would have been if we had had to so suddenly give up our dog. So, he did what he did best: he made a deal and, by doing so, he protected me from suffering a crushing loss.

Smiling through the tears, I found myself beyond negative thoughts. Releasing them, I discovered a wealth of happy experiences I'd shared with my father. I cherished our unique relationship. I am the richer for it.

The tears keep coming, and with them, relief. It wasn't the same kind of relief I'd experienced when he died, and I was grateful for that. This time, I was relieved to know that he truly loved me. What my sisters said - that he hated all of us and didn't really want us - wasn't true. I'd always believed that he did in fact love us even if he couldn't always show it as clearly as he had on the morning he saved Blackie for me.

Now I knew that I had been right. As my tears washed over me, I felt cleansed and happy, knowing that I can be at peace with his memory. I understand he'd had his own fears, that he sometimes he felt betrayed by us - within him was a residue of painful memories from his own childhood. In the 86 years he was alive, he rarely spoke of his own father but chose to hide his pain. How sad for him.

Dad, I want you to know that I understand now, and I'm happy that you have found your peace. I've finally come to terms with our relationship, and now you too share my "ENCHANTED SELF."

How Can You Relate To This Story?

This magnificent story of grieving and finding peace speaks eloquently to the part of each of us that needs to finish a dialogue. Now you have an opportunity to finish your own dialogues – to reach out through writing. Maybe you'll show your words to the person with whom you have an unfinished conversation, or maybe you'll keep them to yourself, in which case writing will have been a cleansing process for you.

Have you known someone whose goodness or personal struggles you've recognized or acknowledged only after the passage of time? Can you now see that this person had been a good friend to you? Take some time now to tell this person what time and distance has helped you see, what you know feel and understand about him or her.

This cleansing process is so personal and private that some of you may prefer not to write your message. As a psychologist, I've seen people who are unable to write, sit and talk to an empty chair in which they imagine the person they want to address is sitting.

Others prefer to write a letter that they then hide or destroy. If you're writing to someone very important in your life, like an ex-lover, or someone who is still alive, you may well be concerned about privacy issues. If so, share your thoughts and words in a very private way. But find a way to speak your mind. Speaking or writing the words in your heart will not only cleanse you but will release your psychic energies so that you will be able to live a more emotionally free and comfortable life.

HARMONIZING

The Peddler Who Came Through Town
(This story is a gift to me from a colleague, Dr. Art Kovacs)

In a small town in Eastern Europe, there lived three musicians – a flutist, a harpsichordist, and a violinist. After Shabbos, they always gathered in the shul to play beautiful music together. Everyone in the village came to hear them. Shabbos was their day of rest – heaven on earth. They were always sad to see it go. The music helped ease the transition from the blessed seventh day to the workaday week, full of stress, strain, and discomfort.

In time, the flutist, who was the oldest of the musicians, grew sick and died. Everyone was terribly sad. On the first Shabbos after his funeral, his two friends gathered at the shul to play. But their music fell flat. It filled the shul and all the congregants with sadness.

One day, a traveling peddler came through the shtetl selling pots and pans, fabric, thread, and other odds and ends. A town elder, picking among the wares for sale, noticed something sticking out of the peddler's sack and asked what it was.

"Why that's my flute," the peddler said.

"Well," said the elder, "in that case, I beg you to stay for Shabbos. Every Saturday night, when Shabbos is over, we gather for music in the shul. And we so need a flute player!" The invitation surprised the peddler. He knew he should move on to the next town. But what if it was far away? What if bandits lurked in the forest on the way there? Facing so many possible dangers and hardships, the peddler agreed to stay.

He was wined and dined in the home of the town's richest man. As Shabbos drew to a close, the peddler was escorted to the shul to meet the other two musicians. Briefly they conferred about the music, and then they began to play.

But to everyone's horror, the music sounded terrible! The notes clashed, the rhythm was disjointed. Everyone who heard wanted to cringe and cover his ears. "Stop!" Someone cried finally. "Stop the flute player! He's no good. He makes the others sound terrible."

But the Rabbi said, "No, no. The other two musicians must stop playing. Let our guest play alone." The harpsichordist and violinist lay down their instruments. In the middle of the peddler's solo, the roof of the shul began to open, slowly exposing the star-filled heavens. To everyone's amazement, his song was in perfect harmony with the heavenly host.

How Can You Relate To This Story?

This story reminds us that someone who appears out of synch with other people may be in perfect harmony with the universe. Dr. Kovacs said he gave me this story to acknowledge my efforts to share THE ENCHANTED SELF. He especially appreciated my efforts to teach other clinicians, as well as the public, to focus on what is right with each of us rather than what is wrong.

It's a universal story. All of us harbor beliefs that make perfect sense to us, yet if we talk to others about them, we meet with resistance or indifference. For example, we may believe that our family needs to eat more healthfully, or that we need to convince a loved one to quit smoking. Yet when we express these desires, we feel shut out – or, even worse, belittled and insulted. It's heartening to know, as the story reminds us, that our own "truth" – if heard in the spirit in which we intend it – could open the heavens above.

Has anyone ever given you a gift like the gift Dr. Kovacs gave to me?

* Or have you ever given a gift to someone else in recognition of their own sense of value, or complimented them, or supported them in their pursuit of the "truth" even if it differs from yours? Take some time to see what comes to mind and write it down. Don't forget, we all need to feel that we are in harmony – that our song is worth singing and is in tune with the universe. One of the most welcome gifts that we can give each other is the gift of recognition.

HELPING

The Japanese Ambassador

One Saturday morning, while I was listening to "All Things Considered" on public radio, the program did a special report on a Japanese ambassador who had lived in Lithuania during World War II. When it became clear that Hitler was out to destroy Jews, the ambassador had been bombarded with requests for visas from Lithuanian Jews.

He wrote to the Japanese government three times requesting permission to grant visas, and three times he was turned down. The ambassador then discussed the situation with his wife, and for two days they agonized over what to do. "These people need help," he told her, "and if I don't help them, no one will, and they may die." His wife encouraged him to come to the Jews' aid, and his five-year-old son also begged him to do so.

Since he did not have official visa documents, the ambassador took it upon himself to handwrite the visas for as many Jewish people as he could over the next few months. He worked 12 hours a day, and his hand went into spasms repeatedly from fatigue. At night, his wife would massage his hands and try to generally restore him so he could continue his task the next day. This went on for months, and it is estimated that 5,000 to 20,000 Jews were saved because of his efforts.

Eventually the ambassador was recalled to Japan. Although he subsequently was appointed to several other government posts, eventually he was forced out of government service, probably because he had disobeyed orders and had helped the very people whom Japan, as an ally of Hitler, was trying to eradicate.

Now his son was talking about him on the radio because the former ambassador was going to be honored, and it was clear that neither the son nor the father had any regrets about what they had done. The interviewer asked the son if his father's good deeds had anything to do with the fact that these people were Jewish. "No," he said. "He did this just because they were suffering. They were frightened, and they needed help. He would have done the same for anyone else."

Each member of the family had in fact been dedicated to the task in whatever way he or she could handle. The five-year-old boy, who had seen frightened Jewish children clutching their parents' hands, had pleaded with his Dad to help them, while his mother did her best to revitalize her husband and kept the family together. All of them were invested in a kindness that went beyond any consideration of personal reward. That kindness had lifelong repercussions for the father, costing him his career, yet even had he known that, "he would have done it unhesitatingly," said the son.

❋ What would you do for anyone, just because the person needed help? For example, would you stop along the road to help in an emergency? What else?

❋ Has anyone ever helped you in a special way that you didn't expect?

❋ How can we teach our children to have the courage to be truly kind?

❋ What can you do over the next few weeks to bring more kindness into the world?

LAUGHING

How Could Timmie Disappear?
Bernice Becker

The Wednesday before Thanksgiving, I'm usually at the supermarket buying bags of food, and then in the kitchen, preparing for the holiday. But this Wednesday, I sat in my lounge chair sipping amaretto-flavored coffee. The short, hectic workweek was over, and the shopping – some nuts, fruit, cheese, wine, and pecan pies – was done. Yes, Thanksgiving would be very different this year.

Instead of hosting the meal, we were going to be guests at the home of our married daughter Barbara, her husband Russell, and our six-month-old granddaughter, Jessica. Russell's parents would be there, too.

Harry, my husband, and Diane, our ten-year-old daughter, now an excited young aunt, and I were planning to leave Thursday morning to arrive in Beverly, where they lived, by one o'clock. Since we were sleeping at our daughter's we didn't have to over-pack. Our only ordeal was to get Timmie, our cat, to the vet for boarding until our return on Friday.

I'm a cat lover. We'd had many cats through the years, and I had indulged them all. But Timmie was the most demanding. He was also high strung. Because we had recently moved to Westfield from Norwalk,

Connecticut this would be Timmie's first encounter with the animal hospital and we were concerned about him.

After dinner Wednesday, Harry, Diane and I managed to get our reluctant and angry pet into his traveling case. He hated to leave home because he knew we were going away. Hoping to appease him, I put his favorite rubber half chewed up mouse and the food he liked in a bag.

For three miles, he snarled, talked, cried, growled and meowed. I kept assuring him we loved him and would come back soon. But inside the animal hospital, Timmie grew frightened and became very silent. Check-in took only a few minutes – we had to leave our names and phone number, and the number of a neighbor in case of emergency – but Timmie was so quiet that I feared he had passed out. We apologized once more for leaving him, and said our good-byes.

Thanksgiving Day was like a dream – good company, fabulous food, interesting conversation, and adorable Jessica, who behaved like a perfect lady and didn't overeat. (I wish I could say the same for the rest of us.) We all marveled at how much she'd grown. Even the friendly rivalry between Russell's mother and myself over who would hold the baby most amused us. (She won.) Friday, the day we had to leave to drive home, arrived all too soon.

Back in Westfield, we headed immediately to rescue Timmie. The woman at the desk looked through a large appointment book for what seemed like a very long time. Finally I asked, "What is taking so long?"

"I have no cat named Timmie," she said.

"That's impossible," I told her. "We checked him in on Wednesday evening."

"Are you sure Timmie is a cat and not a dog?" she asked. We were flabbergasted.

"How could you ask such a crazy question?" Diane blurted out.

Agitated, the woman said, "Well, we do have a dog named Timmie who was also brought in Wednesday evening…"

"Look," I said. "I'm going to check every cage until we find our cat. He has to be here."

But we saw no sign of him. I had just started to panic when I heard a familiar howling, and the sound of a body being thrown against a cage door.

Sure enough, there was Timmie, furious and frightened – and imprisoned for way too long. "He must have heard us and recognized our smell," my husband said.

"Here's the problem," said Diane, pointing to the sign above Timmie's cage – which read HARRY, my husband's name, in big, black letters. Mystery solved.

We explained the mix-up to the woman at the desk. She looked as relieved as Timmie did as he leaped into his carrying case. We paid the fee and chuckled the whole way home.

When we got to our driveway, we let Harry – I mean Timmie – out. He ran to the bushes to hide – our punishment for having treated him so badly. Later we heard crying and scratching at the front door. When I opened it, he rushed in and went right to his bowl. I'd left him a peace offering: a cut-up chunk of white meat turkey – his favorite.

He settled down to enjoy his repast. I could hear him purring. Then he paused, came over to me, and rubbed himself against my leg. I understood him perfectly. "Thank you," he said. "And don't worry, I forgive you. After all, you are only human."

How Can You Relate To This Story?

I hope you enjoyed the story of Timmie the missing cat as much as I did. Imagine how confused Timmie must have been at the vet's! But tragedy was averted, and a distressing story was transformed into a humorous one. All of us have suffered through moments of dread, anxiety or confusion which, if we were lucky, was resolved happily. Memory works in mysterious ways. Time often distills even painful feelings, leaving us with stories we love to tell again and again.

* *Can you remember a distressing moment from your life that in time became funny to think about and tell to others? Don't worry about making it into a formal story; just put down the details as best you can.*

✸ If you haven't told this story in a while, find someone who will enjoy hearing it so you can have the pleasure of laughing together.

LEARNING

<u>That Ain't Worth Nothin'</u>

When my dad was about five or six years old, living on Redfield Street in New Haven, Connecticut, he was eager as the next fellow to find a shiny penny or anything else of value. He lived in a neighborhood of immigrants, or greenhorns as they were called, and money was so tight that treats for children were almost unheard of. But children were resourceful. They knew that one way to scrounge up a penny to put in their pockets was to turn in a returnable bottle – that is, if they could find one. Since most families hoarded their own returns, strays were hard to come by.

One day my father was playing in the street with a neighborhood friend who was a year or two older than my dad. As they ran through the gutters with a stick and a ball, they spotted a bottle. My dad was the first to pounce upon it, dropping his stick in his eagerness to hold it. "Oh, Harry, don't bother with that bottle," his friend said. "That bottle ain't worth nothin'."

"But it's a returnable," my dad said. "It could be worth at least a penny and I want that penny."

"That bottle ain't worth nothin' to you, Harry," the other boy said. "Get rid of it and let's play." My dad clutched the bottle. "It ain't worth nothin' to you, Harry!" The boy said again. Finally, my father dropped the bottle and picked up his stick, ready to resume play. In an instant, his friend snatched the bottle. "See you tomorrow, Harry!" he yelled, as he ran down the block. "I gotta return this."

"But you said it wasn't worth anything," my father cried out. "You said that!"

"Ain't worth nothin' to you, Harry," the boy called over his shoulder as he disappeared around the block, "but to me it's worth a penny and I'm going for it now!"

Bereft, my father stood there – without his playmate, without the bottle, and without the shiny penny he'd anticipated pocketing. It's a sad story – but over the years, my family has come to think of it as a learning story. My father told it often when he thought that one of us was being taken advantage of. It was his way of reminding us that we needed to think clearly and act in our own best interest. It also taught us that people who appear selfless sometimes aren't. We need to stay alert, use logic, and remain immune from the influences of others.

How Can You Relate To This Story?

Have you ever lost an opportunity? Did someone influence you in a negative way, and you realized it only in retrospect? Did you ever make a decision without taking the time you needed to determine what would be best for you?

It's not always easy to seize opportunities when they arise. To do so, we need not only to think logically, but to get help from those will respond in a disinterested or neutral way. For example, my dad would have been smarter had he said to his friend, "I'll ask my mother if this bottle is worth something – she'll know – and if it ain't, then I'll throw it out."

❋ *If you've thought of an episode when you didn't act in your own best interests, don't just dwell on it – write down what you might have thought or what you might have done that would have served you better.*

❋ *Can you recall an incident that happened in the past when you were pleased that you had listened to your own better judgment? Sometimes we are called upon to make subtle distinctions, particularly in the contest of relationships. Your spouse may discourage you from doing something that feels right to you simply because his view of the world is so different from yours. I remember a time, for example, when I decided I had just had it with our dishwasher. It didn't really clean the dishes very well, and it was annoying to load and unload. My husband had no interest in buying a new machine. He was concerned about the money, and he didn't want to purchase a new appliance before we absolutely needed to – which, in his* opinion, would occur when the dishwasher wouldn't work at all.

Of course, I was the one loading and unloading the dishwasher each day, and experiencing daily aggravation each time to I had to scrub off the food that had not been rinsed away. He tried to persuade me that his position was right, and I listened, but I also had personal discussions with myself. Maybe a new dishwasher wasn't worth anything to my husband, but the comfort of a new one was important to me.

❋ How about you? Can you remember a time when you took your own best advice despite what others were saying? Write your experience here.

LIVING

Life At A Dharma Center: Challenging, Rewarding, and Not Easy!
Sherri Rosen

Living at Karme Choling Buddhist Retreat Center for two years was like having your feet weighted down in tar in a room full of mirrors. I couldn't escape, and everywhere I looked, I saw myself in others.

Many times I wanted to leave because it became so claustrophobic. Living with 60 people, seeing them everyday, and having programs with them all the time, there was no escape. I felt as if I was on the spot constantly. Whenever I would get agitated, angry, or sad, I would look at the people with whom I was dealing and I'd see the same feelings reflected in their faces. Even if you had just broken up with your lover, you still had to see him or her everyday – you had to deal with each other whether you liked it or not. Of course, we all had our own little hiding places. But even that didn't always work.

Everyone had a daily job, seven days a week. Then there was also extra work that took up approximately five hours a week, to clean the center and assist in setting up programs. Sometimes entire days would go by and I would realize that I hadn't practiced yoga because I was working so hard. Yet overall, I was able to practice at the center more than I would have at home because I didn't have a job to go to or a family to care for. All our basic needs – food, clothing, shelter, and medical care – were seen to.

Karme Choling is situated on 500 acres of rolling hills in Barnet, Vermont, just three hours south of Montreal. From the outside, the retreat center, a converted farmhouse, blends in with the New England countryside. But step inside and you're transported into another world. The five shrine rooms are adorned with vibrant reds, greens, blues and golds, and huge pictures of the Buddha and other deities of Tibetan Buddhism command your attention.

The center was founded by Chogyam Trungpa twenty-eight years ago. He had escaped from the Chinese in Tibet in 1959, was educated in England, shed his robes, took an English wife, and came to the United States, bringing the teachings of Hinyana, Mahayana and Vajrayana Buddhism to the West. As I understand the different sects, Hinyana involves cleaning up your own act so that you can go on to help others, Mahayana involves letting go of your own ego in order to help others become enlightened, and Vajrayana is the direct path to enlightenment. In the short time Trungpa was in the West, he gave us many gifts and showed us that there were other ways of looking at the world. Wherever he went he created controversy, much of which remains today. But his primary teaching to us Westerners was simply this: Wake UP!

Living at Karme Choling was a transformative experience for me, though I didn't realize it until I returned to New York City a year ago. The center functioned as a container for all of us, and showed me how to use that container for myself – how to make myself into that container. What I mean is that I learned that I didn't have to be so reactive to people; I didn't have to allow other people to have power over me. People could go through their own trips and I didn't have to take on their experiences. Instead, I could hold my feelings, thoughts, emotions within and just let them go.

For instance, a friend grew angry at me for something she thought she heard me say. Ordinarily, I would have responded in anger, but after my stay at the center, I didn't. I took a deep breath, let go, and told her calmly and patiently what I meant.

One of my happiest recollections took place in the kitchen just before Shambhala Day, the Tibetan New Year. The head cook had received permission to play some klezmer music as we prepared for the holiday. Listening to the music, I began to dance, and within moments the whole staff was dancing, too. It truly was joyous and brought such delight to the children.

Another delightful experience was sitting on the floor with a delicious, soft, cuddly newborn baby sleeping in my arms in the shrine room. As I listened to teachings on gentleness and kindness, I would first look down at the baby, then at the other people in the shrine room, and finally at the pictures of Buddha on the wall. I felt so grateful to be alive.

My stay at the center showed me how to transform passion into compassion; how to be more flexible; and to accept people as they are, not the way I would like them to be - a profound transformation. I even discovered that I had the ability to heal others, that my container was able to take in the power of healing and let it flow into others. As a result, I have been studying healing for the past year and practicing in New York City, where it is most needed.

Now I know that the teachings will always be a part of me – they surface constantly in how I treat others and myself, and by guiding me to the livelihood I will pursue. I had received the most blessed gift of all from being in Trungpa's retreat: Gratefulness. I awaken to each new day and accept the gift of being human. Trungpa called this "ordinary magic."

How Can You Relate To This Story?

I found this story moving. It is about the trials and tribulations we encounter when we learn to accept the gift of being human. I love the term "ordinary magic," which hints at much of the same mystery.

When we create "Recipes for Enchantment" on a daily basis, we take the ordinary doings of everyday life and combine them with the magic of our positive, personal feelings and thoughts in such a way that the result can never be recreated. Each day's weather is unique – and so is our agenda for the day, our energy level, how well we're feeling, what we're wearing, and how much money we have in our pocket. We wake up each morning to different tasks and purposes. And to each day we bring diverse memories and attitudes about what we're doing.

Take Sherry's story as an opportunity to think about how "ordinary magic" can happen in your life. I had the opportunity to do this just recently. Housebound during a snowstorm, I found myself feeling particularly warm and contented with my life. The coffee tasted good; the cats were fun to play with; the house looked relatively clean; I had no chores to obsess about; my e-mail was interesting; I found some new sites to visit on the web; and the phone rang frequently so I had the opportunity to talk to several friends and family members, which prevented me from feeling alone. Within my contained circumstances, I felt serene and comfortable all day. It could have turned out differently. I could have spent the day dwelling on all of the irritations in my life, and on the lack of joy. But instead, I felt hopeful. All alone, with few outside distractions, I could still achieve "ordinary magic."

✻ Take some time to describe a day of "ordinary magic" in your life. If you have trouble coming up with a day, think of an evening, an hour, or even a few minutes during which you felt whole, comfortable with yourself, at ease, and centered in your life.

✳ List those factors that contributed to this special day or hour. Did you do anything special to achieve this "ordinary magic?" List these steps here. Did any of your positive thoughts or feelings augment your peaceful feelings? If so, list them, too.

Can you integrate this experience into the larger story of your life? In other words does this incident of "ordinary magic" reflect strengths, talents, potential or coping skills that you absorbed and made your own earlier in your life? For me, the fact that I had been alone a great deal as a child - doing homework, practicing the violin, and cleaning up in an empty house - prepared me for my housebound day during the snowstorm. Over the past few years, I have made a conscious effort to view my early days not as lonely times but as opportunities. I learned to enjoy being close to myself and had the chance to discover my own inner stride and inner rhythm. I see this capacity as a real talent rather than as a reflection of personal despair. For example, instead of wishing that I had brothers or sisters when I was young, or that my parents were home more often, I understand my childhood as a time during which I discovered my personal resiliency and learned to honor myself as an individual who could make use of private time.

❋ *Can you reinterpret some experiences in your past in this new way? If so, write about your new understanding.*

LOVING

Grandma Sadie's Blintzes
Ellen Saposnik

Everything my Grandma Sadie cooked and baked was the best! She could turn a simple dish into something heavenly. One of my favorites was potato blintzes, a crepe-like dough with a peppery-potato filling. Although she lived alone, Sadie would whip up vast quantities of blintzes for her only granddaughter (me!), using her special frying pan. We are a kosher family and blintzes, fried in margarine or butter, are a delectable dairy dinner. Sadie took a great deal of pride in everything she prepared for the family – that's just how she was – and so each package contained four to six perfect blintzes wrapped in freezer paper meticulously dated to ensure we would eat the older ones first. She continued to make the family blintzes until late April 1983 when she suffered a stroke. After three weeks in intensive care, Sadie left us. With her passing, a great light in my life was extinguished. At the time I was almost eight months pregnant with my second child, Noah Seth, who was lovingly named for the great-grandmother he would never know.

All that I had left of Sadie were the blintzes in the freezer. After several weeks of quiet disbelief and mourning, my mother reminded me to start eating the blintzes before they became too old to enjoy. I did as she instructed and each package, carefully labeled in Sadie's own handwriting, was consumed with silent reverence. Finally, there was only one package left. Although I had Sadie's recipe, I know that an era had passed. When I cooked the last of the blintzes, I was careful to save the freezer paper with her handwriting. Twelve years later, I still cherish it. I keep it in my recipe box where I hope it will impart its loving magic to the meals that will be prepared from my recipes for generations to come. Good-bye, Grandma Sadie. Thanks for the blintzes and so much love! Perhaps YOU would like to try Sadie's blintzes. Here is the recipe. (Serves 4 to 6):

INGREDIENTS

- ♦ 1 egg, beaten
- ♦ 1 cup of water
- ♦ 1 cup of all-purpose flour
- ♦ 2 large potatoes, peeled, boiled and mashed
- ♦ butter or margarine
- ♦ salt and pepper to taste
- ♦ Optional - 1 medium white onion, diced and pan fried in butter until clear.

BLINTZE LEAVES

Beat one egg with one cup of water. Add one cup of all-purpose flour and pinch of salt. Mix until there are no lumps. Using a 7-$\frac{1}{2}$ or 8-inch frying pan, rub the bottom and sides with butter or margarine. Heat the pan over medium heat and pour 2-3 tablespoons of batter into the center of the pan. Swirl the pan until entire bottom of the pan has a thin layer of batter. Cook until edges start to come away from the sides and the blintz leaf appears cooked. Flip out of the pan onto paper towel. Only one side is cooked in the frying pan.

POTATO FILLING
Peel and boil 2 large potatoes. When cooked, mash and add salt and pepper to taste. Cooked onions can be added if desired.

TO ASSEMBLE
Put one tablespoon of potato filling into the bottom half of each blintz leaf. Fold up from the bottom, fold in the two sides, and continue to roll. Blintzes can be frozen before they are fried. Fry in butter or margarine and ENJOY!

How Can You Relate To This Story?

Can you think of special foods that you associate with being loved? For example I remember the chocolate cupcakes with rich chocolate frosting swirled on top that my grandmother always had waiting for me when I visited, even when I was "grown up." It was a wonderful feeling to be offered a rich chocolate cupcake and a glass of milk even at 25. There was no one else in the world who would give me that kind of treat. Even my mother would not have indulged me, as she was more conscious of me keeping my trim, youthful figure than was my grandmother.

* *Jot down some of your memories of these favorite foods and the circumstances surrounding them.*

* *Was there a special recipe or recipes? Jot it down here.*

MENTORING

The Sweet Touch of Mr. Zuckerman
Tzvia Singer

When I was a youngster, there was a special man in my life who helped me develop and believe in myself. His name was Mr. Zuckerman. When I met him, Mr. Zuckerman was living in New Haven's Hebrew Home for the Aged. He'd become blind in his forties and needed daily assistance.

Mr. Zuckerman had many wonderful qualities. He was brave, proud, self-respecting, self-sufficient, generous and intuitive, but he also accepted kindness, help and caring. He rejected sympathy, feeling that his senses were heightened as compensation for his blindness. As a resident of the Home, he was the soul of kindness toward the community. In one of his many helpful roles, he tutored children. I was fortunate enough to be one of these children, a recipient of his bounty and limitless love.

Would you believe me if I told you that he was tremendous fun to be with? Sometimes, he'd offer to accompany me to the playground so I could swing on the jungle gym with the other children. "I can do that any time," I'd say to him. "I can't always talk to you."

Yes, it was true: I'd rather be with him than go to the park. Spending time with him was as precious as hanging out with my friends, or eating ice cream. One hot summer afternoon I walked into the Home to meet him, and found him dressed in long pants and his undershirt. He was so embarrassed to be seen this way! I assured him that I didn't mind, but he had so much self-respect and modesty that he went right to his closet for a shirt. In fact, he was a natty dresser, and always immaculate. I remember his summer outfit best: a straw hat and a lightweight suit. And his shoes were always shined.

What did I talk to him about? Most often, I told him what had happened to me that day, and what had hurt me. He listened carefully, as if he were glad that I was unburdening my heart to him. He didn't advise me. Although he encouraged me to refrain from speaking negatively about my family, he listened if I felt that I needed to complain about them, and shared my pain.

One day I particularly remember. He asked if he could "see me." I didn't understand how this would be possible. But he told me that if he gently rubbed the palm of his hand over my face, he would know what I looked like. His soft, delicate fingers gingerly touching my brow and running across my closed eyes, nose, chin and cheeks felt as warm as a summer breeze. He declared me beautiful.

I declare him beautiful. He influenced my life and development in profoundly positive ways and I hope that his gentle courage and wisdom will similarly affect you!

How Can You Relate To This Story?

I also had a very special mentor in my life when I was growing up. I met him when I was 15; unfortunately, he passed away when I was 21.

I met Mr. Del Sylvester through my father, who was Superintendent of Schools in Norwalk, Connecticut. After hearing my father speak at several Board of Education meetings, Mr. Sylvester, who was then 70 years young, called and invited my entire family to his home for cocktails. His was the courage not to wait until he was formally introduced but to take a risk and reach out to others. My mother was a little surprised by his call, but said that he sounded sincere. We all agreed that we should go.

What an entryway into a joyful life that visit proved!

The Sylvesters lived in simple graciousness. Their home was filled not only with comfortable chairs and couches, but also with books and music. They even owned a small rowboat, and cultivated a beautiful Japanese garden that Mr. Sylvester worked on during the last few years of his life. Our discussion during our first meeting ranged from gourmet foods and God's love to questions about how American democracy could really come into its own as a great, permanent system. We had many more discussions after this, all interspersed with good humor. Sometimes we met in their comfortable living room overlooking the bay. We also met at restaurants. In fact, Mr. Sylvester took us to our first French and Swedish restaurants. We'd never before had wine with a meal except as part of a Jewish ceremony. But with Mr. Sylvester, we were learning many new things.

Mr. Sylvester and his wife had great hope for humanity. They believed that people could fill their lives with joy and meaning, and care about each other at the same time. Their work reflected these beliefs: Mrs. Sylvester taught the handicapped. On many occasions, her former students would come to visit, often with their spouses and children. They were treated like dear friends, just as we were, with warmth, sincerity, hospitality and dignity.

Mr. Sylvester was a beacon for my entire family. He advised my father about school and politics, and my mother about gourmet foods. He always encouraged me to follow my dreams. He wanted me to use my mind and to study the great philosophers of the world. He also urged me to play and have fun, to learn to ski, travel, and meet people. He taught me to cherish all of life's riches. His was the love of a special grandfather.

Mr. Sylvester died on the weekend that President Kennedy was assassinated, though he was unaware of the event. It would have been profoundly painful for him to have known.

Hardly a day of my life has gone by since Mr. Sylvester's death that I haven't thought about him and haven't been nourished by him. Certainly, his belief in me as a young person has supported me. Whenever I think about living a life rather than just moving through a life, I feel the comfort of his friendship.

✺ Can you recall a mentor in your life? He or she may have been a religious schoolteacher, a scout leader, a neighbor, one of your parents or even a child who helped you develop into the person you are today. Here's a golden opportunity to talk about this person, and to reflect on what he or she did for you. If that person is still alive, I hope that recalling his or her influence and writing about it will encourage you to get back in touch through a card or phone call.

✺ If you can't think of someone who played a direct role in your life, write about a person you came to know by reading about him or her, or about someone in the public eye who has impressed you. It may be someone well known like President Lincoln, or a fictional character like Nancy Drew – or maybe a special neighbor down the street. I'm sure that there are people who have taught you important lessons. Take some time to reminisce about any of them and what they did for you.

PRAYING

Learning From Street Children

Marilyn Rocky, Chairman and Director of Project Child Hope, tells a wonderful story about two street children she met when she was in Brazil on business.

She and a colleague, out for dinner, found themselves walking through Rio de Janeiro's Copacabana – a famous tourist beach which is also home to thousands of street children who come to beg and sell trinkets. They noticed two malnourished boys, about six and eight, begging on the street. Both were thin and had skin disorders clearly associated with poor nutrition. "My colleague and I decided to invite these children to come with us to an outdoor café so we could buy them a meal," Marilyn says. "Because neither of us spoke Portuguese, we just gestured, and they understood. Smiling and excited, they came with us."

"Clearly, the other patrons and waiters were not happy to see these little boys. But we insisted that they sit with us. Each of the boys ordered a plate of spaghetti and an orange soda. Then they waited patiently until the food came, which took quite some time."

Marilyn and her friend, hungry after a long day of work, couldn't wait to dig in. But the boys stopped them, gesturing for the women to wait. Confused, they watched as each boy put his head down, put his hands together in prayer, and said grace. Marilyn and her friend looked at each other in awe. "It was such a humbling moment," Marilyn recalls. "These are kids who struggle every day to survive, yet their own spirituality was more important than food."

Feeling uplifted, she and her friend joined the boys in saying grace and when it was over, they all dived into the food, enjoying every bite.

How Can You Relate To This Story?

What a sacred moment in time these little street boys were able to provide for Marilyn and her friend! How humbling it was for them to be mentored by children who own nothing, and who are chronically hungry, yet still honor the Divine.

❈ *Can you think of a time in your life when you were suddenly jarred out of complacency or indifference by another person or living creature who helped regain a state of grace? Sometimes a beloved dog or cat who accepts us even when we're in a bad mood can help us realize how insular we are and how far from the divine path we have strayed.*

PRETENDING

The Claydigger Finds a Diamond

This story is loosely based on a story of the great Hasidic master, Rabbi Nachman.

There was once a poor claydigger who spent his days digging clay and selling it. Though the job itself was trying, he enjoyed it. And he was ever on the alert in case a trinket lay buried in the clay. Sure enough, one day he unearthed the most amazing treasure: a huge diamond. He knew it must be worth a fortune. The local jeweler confirmed his suspicions – no one in his eastern European village would be able to buy it. He would have to take it to London if he wished to receive fair value for it.

He had never traveled more than a few miles beyond his village and he certainly didn't have the money for a journey on the high seas. However, he decided to stake his life on this diamond. Selling all his possessions, he traveled to the port city. There he found a captain who said, upon seeing the giant diamond, "You're a sure bet."

The claydigger was ushered into a first-class cabin with a window looking out on the sea. As the days passed and the waves rocked the ship up and down, the claydigger would sit in his cabin gazing with joy at his diamond. At mealtimes, he placed it on his table so he could stare at it as he ate.

One day after a hearty meal, the claydigger took a nap. While he was sleeping, the cabin boy entered his cabin to clear off the lunch table. To clean the tablecloth, he shook it out the window. All the crumbs fell into the water – along with the diamond.

When the claydigger woke up, he was bereft. Not only had he lost his entire fortune, but he felt sure that captain would certainly murder him for the price of the boat ticket. Inescapable dread filled his soul.

It was at this very moment that he made the greatest decision of his life. At the moment of his greatest unhappiness and hopelessness, he decided he would pretend to be happy. He would act as if nothing at all had happened.

Incredibly, the feat was easier to pull off than he realized. When the captain visited with him in his cabin, the claydigger would listen to the captain's stories, grinning and chuckling as he always had upon hearing of the captain's adventures in exotic lands. Though the claydigger felt tortured inside, he didn't let it show. The captain had no idea that anything had changed.

One day the captain said, "My friend, you are a wealthy man and I need to ask you a favor. Will you cosign an agreement with me? I'm buying a large quantity of produce to sell in London and I'm afraid that the buyers will suspect my signature. But if you will cosign, their fears will be assuaged. I'm sure that I can make a large profit and will repay you handsomely."

Certainly the claydigger felt that it was to his advantage to sign. He had nothing to lose and everything to gain.

But imagine his surprise when, soon after transacting their business in London, the captain dropped dead! Since the claydigger's signature was already on the bill of sale, he legally owned the produce and was able to sell it for much more money than the diamond had been worth.

The claydigger then returned to his village with his pockets full of gold. To paraphrase what Rabbi Nachman would say, "He only came into his own because he kept his fears to himself and found a way to be happy."

How Can You Relate To This Story?

* *Have you ever known in your heart that you had to behave as if everything was going to be all right even though the sky appeared to be falling? Read my story and then tell yours.*

I had such an experience. What helped me through it was relying on the support and assistance from loved ones.

The summer after my senior year of college, I began a Master's degree in education at a prestigious university. I was filled with enthusiasm and eagerness – not only would I get six credits under my belt, but I'd also have actual experience in the third- and fourth-grade classrooms.

But three weeks into the program, several trainees were asked to leave – including me! Our supervisors had determined that we were not "teacher material." Specifically, I was told that I was too stiff and nervous with the children and had not been able to take command of the classroom quickly enough.

In utter despair, I left. When I arrived home, my parents sat me down and said, "We don't know what happened, but we absolutely believe that you will make a good teacher. We've seen you interact with children for years and you've always been warm, sensitive, and caring. You ask good questions, explain things well, and make children feel very special." Then my dad said, "What you should do now is apply to another teacher training program for this fall."

I was torn. On one hand, I had believed that not only was I intuitively a good teacher but also that I would be successful in whatever work I decided to do. On the other hand, my supervisors had made a judgment about me. Perhaps they saw things in me my parents and I were unable to see. Maybe I should just give up, I thought to myself.

When I think back to this period of my life, I felt as if other people were trampling on my destiny. Thankfully, I had the support of my parents, for without them I wasn't as strong as the claydigger. With their encouragement, I began interviewing at and applying to several schools of education - and was accepted to every one. Because I still felt wounded by my earlier evaluations, I chose the school at which I felt most comfortable. By early September, I enrolled in its Master's program in education. My courage began to return.

That year turned out to be one of the most gratifying academic experiences I ever had. My wonderful advisor, Dr. Alice B. Crossley encouraged me and my colleagues to do a small group thesis in "Synectics: A Creative Thinking Approach to Invention Solving." I excelled at student teaching, and made connections with various professors so that within two years I was at Boston University working on my doctorate. Soon thereafter, I found a wonderful teaching job in Concord, Massachusetts.

This experience helped me learn that there are many ways that we become courageous and fulfill out destinies.

❀ Can you think of a time when you made a leap of faith, or kept faith with yourself? These are the moments that bring fire to our souls and help remind us that we are not weaklings. They also bear witness to the passionate core within each one of us. We not only have good instincts and survivor skills, but we also know to what we are entitled, what is rightfully ours. It was rightfully mine to become a teacher - and this *proved the first step along a long and rewarding career path for me. You can begin by making a list here of some of the things that are rightfully yours.*

It can often be fun to share stories of our leaps of faith in a group – these are the stories that add fire to our souls and help remind us that we are not weaklings. Why don't you consider having some friends over some night and around snacks and sitting comfortably, share some of your leap of faith stories. I can guarantee you'll have a fun evening and feel inspired by the shared experience.

❋ *To get ready for your evening of inspiration, you can warm up by making a list here of some of the things that are rightfully yours and any related strength that you've witnessed in yourself as you held on to what is rightfully yours.*

REMINISCING

Not The Same Old Story
Sylvia Schultz Margolin

The older I become, the more I realize the importance of sharing my own growing up years with Molly, my four and a half-year-old granddaughter. Although the events I recount to her seem quite ordinary to me, to Molly they sound like magical adventures.

Molly lives in Michigan. When my husband and I visit, she always says, "Tell me a story." I love to tell stories, so her request is easy to gratify. Mostly, I spin imaginary tales of princes, castles, animals, and enchanted forests.

But one early morning, when Molly climbed into bed ready for a story, my mind didn't immediately snap to "pretend." Instead, I asked if I could tell her a story about when I was a little girl. Her eyes became big and bright and she bubbled, "Oh yes!"

"Once upon a time, a long time ago," I began, "my daddy owned a shoe store in Newark. He drove the family car to work so that he could close the store early and be home in time for supper. On Saturdays, a big shopping day, when the store was open until 9:00 P.M. My mother would prepare a meal at home – soup, sliced roast, vegetables, and dessert. She would then pack everything into pots and jars, and line paper bags with towels, so that my father could have his meal at work."

"At first my older sister and brother would travel to the store with his food. Then one day – I must have been about eleven – the task became mine. In order to get to my father's store, I had to take two buses. I boarded the first across the street from my home where my mother could see me. The second bus was a transfer stop about two miles away. During the long trip, I held the bag of warm food on my lap. It smelled delicious. Although I recall feeling very grownup, the bus drivers got to know me and always watched out for me. Once I arrived, I walked by myself for one block to the store."

"The stockroom behind my father's store contained a desk, which served as our dinner table, and two chairs. I gave my dad supper and kept his food warm when customers came in. After he finished eating, I would clean up, carefully washing and drying the containers. I also helped Dad with the customers by keeping their little children occupied so he could properly fit their shoes. Sometimes I remained in the back, putting shoes into boxes and organizing the stock room. If business was slow, we would sit at the desk and play casino, or my father would read the paper and I would sit next to him and do my homework. Finally it was time to go home. I would pack things up, my father would lock up for the night, and we would drive home."

Recounting this story to Molly – recalling the time spent with my father, the lessons I learned, and the comfortable love that was mine – made me feel warm all over. Molly was in awe of the fact that I rode on two public buses all by myself because she only takes one bus to school.

Now, whenever I see her, she asks, "Tell me a story about when you rode on a bus by yourself and tell me about your father's shoe store." In my ordinary memory, Molly has found wonder and I have found a treasure. As I relate the story to her, I have the opportunity to visit with my still youthful parents and relive many wonderful moments. Best of all, I can share all this with the next generation.

How Can You Relate To This Story?

Sometimes "simple recollections" are extremely nourishing. I loved when my grandmother told me about how the trolley car with rattan seats would pass near her house – in the summer, the cars were open to the outside – and how she'd ride by herself into downtown Boston to take her piano lessons. This particular story was simple and short, yet hearing it made me feel both loved and connected to a vision of my youthful grandmother which I would never have otherwise known.

* *Write down some "simple recollections" from your own life.*

❋ *Now take an opportunity to write down some "simple recollections" told to you by someone else.*

Over the next few months, invite some people to come together to share their recollections. I guarantee that if someone is courageous enough to start the ball rolling by telling her recollections, everyone else will soon join in.   In no time at all, you will all be talking at once, remembering long-forgotten, wonderful stories. Reciprocal stories help us to connect with each other and also with ourselves. It's like magic.

RENEWING

The House My Great-Grandfather Built

When I was a child, I loved to listen to stories my grandmother told about growing up in Chelsea, Massachusetts. She was refined and beautiful, and I was intrigued by every facet of her life: that she was the oldest of nine children; that her parents employed two live-in maids; that her mother and a seamstress made most of the family's clothes, pressing them with a flat iron that had to be heated on the stove; that when she was older she traveled alone, by trolley, into Boston, to take piano lessons at the Boston Conservatory of Music, and that the house she grew up in had a twin across the street – a house identical in every detail but reversed – where her father's friend, who had designed both houses, lived.

Each room in my grandmother's house had its own magical story. The top floor playroom was huge enough to roughhouse in, and contained a giant reed organ. The kitchen had a tin ceiling that could be rolled back during the holiday of Succoth so that the family could eat under the stars. Great-Grandma and Great-Grandpa would hang fruits and vegetables from a trellis above their heads, and eat all their meals there for a week, talking, as they ate, about the forty years that the Jews had wandered in the desert. My own parents didn't celebrate Succoth, so hearing about Grandma's celebration sounded especially magical to me.

But perhaps her most unbelievable story – which her older brothers confirm as true – happened in the dining room. When my grandmother was sixteen, she developed a terrible stomach ache. The doctor who came to the house diagnosed appendicitis and said that she had to go to the hospital for an operation. But Grandma cried and refused to go. In despair, her father insisted that the doctor perform the surgery at home. After sterilizing the walls and floor, the doctor removed my grandmother's appendix right there, on the dining room table, the one on which her father ate his banquet lunch every day with his children on his knees. I think this story sticks in my mind because it suggests a time when people could control their circumstances in certain ways that are no longer permitted.

One day, after Grandma had been gone for a few years, my husband and I decided to drive to Chelsea with our baby daughter, Jessica. We searched the small streets for what felt like hours until we found our destination – two old houses, one the mirror image of the other. On the front lawn of my Grandma's house was a sign that said, "Alfred Lopez for Councilman – Vote for Him."

With my heart aching, I walked to the front door and rang the bell, hoping that the owners would let me in. The door was opened by a man who didn't look like anyone in my family. Politely, and somewhat sheepishly, he said, "Oh I'd love to show you the house. But it's in such bad shape. For years it's been a boarding house. We just recently bought it and I'm really ashamed to take you upstairs. But if you'd like, I'll show you the first floor."

With great trepidation, I walked through these now gray, run-down rooms that looked so much smaller than they appeared in my imagination. I saw what must have been the parlor and the dining room - though it was hard to imagine the long, elegant dining room table in that dingy room. I asked if I could see the upstairs, but Mr. Lopez kindly but firmly refused. Oh well, I thought, the reed organ must be long gone anyway. But I did see the kitchen where I found the remains of the tin ceiling and the small, now very rusty wheels and track along which it was retracted.

Standing there, I tried to recall all of Grandma's beautiful stories - the meals she described, the aromas, the laughter, the fun, the maids heating hot irons while the seamstresses took measurements. But it was hard.

Several children had accompanied us as we walked from room to room; I assumed they were Mr. Lopez's. Now, as we made our way to the front door, they came with us. I thanked him for sharing his home with me. Just as I was about to leave, he said, out of the blue, "This is a wonderful home. I'm so glad we bought it. It's perfect for my wife and myself and our nine children."

Suddenly I felt tears behind my eyes and a lump in my throat as I realized that my grandmother's childhood home had not been deserted. A new family, also with nine children, was creating their own home within its walls. I felt as if the essence of my family was still inside – as if our love of connection and good conversation and our pleasure at belonging to a tribe had permeated the wood beams themselves, welcoming another family into its loving embrace.

How Can You Relate To This Story?

This true story about my family always moves me. It's a wonderful story of essential renewal. So many times in life, what's right finally does happen. It just may not happen in the way we initially expected. My grandmother's house deserved a family. What a lovely touch that the Divine brought the Lopez's and their nine children to live there. Though they are from a different "tribe," they are a loving family. Sometimes it's hard to see what is essential in life. We grow so accustomed to looking at the trappings.

Have you ever had an experience after which you realized, "What goes around, comes around?" Maybe years after you worked with someone, for instance, that person told you how much she had appreciated you. Perhaps you see in a grandchild qualities which you couldn't appreciate in his parents, or that his parents don't appreciate. I see another example of balance and renewal today. Many young families have decided to take charge by making a stand against the tide of popular culture by choosing to value family time instead. For example, many have rules pertaining to television watching, permitting it only at certain hours or allowing only certain channels to be viewed. This certainly seems to be a reaction to the abundance of media stimulation in our lives, and an attempt to balance it with more meaningful activities.

* Can you think of a story from your own life? If you can't, don't worry. Come back to this story on another occasion. Maybe by then you will have a story to tell about justice, or about someone who made an attempt to provide balance in a tumultuous and unbalanced world.

SAVING

A Soldier's Love for his Family

Once there was a young man who lived in a small town in the United States. He loved his family: his mother, his father, his grandparents, his aunts and uncles, cousins, brothers and sisters. When the Second World War came, he signed up for the armed forces, along with thousands of other young men of his generation. He was frightened and overwhelmed, but determined to give his life, if necessary, for his country.

As his last day at home drew closer, he had many opportunities to say goodbye. Special masses were offered at church, and his family threw a gala goodbye party attended by over 150 family and friends. His mother hugged and kissed him. He watched the tears form in her eyes as his father toasted him. At the train station, he had one last handshake from Dad. He watched his family waving, growing smaller and smaller, as the train pulled out of the station. He was on his way toward the scary unknown of war.

The next several months held many adventures. From some he grew; others were too terrible to even think about. Loving letters from his mother, grandmother, and his favorite aunt, Celia, sustained him. It seemed as if every mail call held a letter for him, with welcome news of his family and town, and reassurance that he was in everyone's prayers.

One night, a terrible battle raged. He and his friends were positioned in the front trenches listening to exploding bombs and artillery. Then tragedy struck. His two best friends in the next trench were felled by bullets and mortally wounded. Before he could register the shock of their death, he felt a searing, intense pain. He himself was hit. He looked toward his back hip. Blood. Blood was pouring out of his body.

But there was no time to attend to his wounds. Certain he was dying, and that he would join his comrades by morning to help them work their way to the heavenly host, he nonetheless fired his gun all night, as best he could.

Dawn came. He looked around. All was eerily quiet. Unbelievably, he was still alive. But was death close? In a matter of moments or hours would he find himself in a hospital bed? Would he lose his limbs? Live out the rest of his life in excruciating pain? He started to explore his back hip where he'd been hit. He felt and he felt. Despite the quantity of dried blood around the wound, it seemed superficial, already beginning to scab. Suddenly he remembered the back pocket of his army pants. That's where he stuffed all the letters from his grandmother, mother and aunt. He removed the letters. And slowly he realized what had happened. A huge bullet was lodged in the now unreadable pages. They had acted like a shield, preventing the bullet from penetrating him. If not for the letters, he would have certainly been killed.

How Can You Relate To This Story?

What an incredible mystical love story!

Have you ever felt the hand of God helping you negotiate your life, moving in the love that you feel for others and they feel for you? I certainly have. I had a series of appendicitis attacks when I was 10 and 11, and because the doctors couldn't find anything wrong with me, they literally turned my mother away when she brought me to the hospital. But my mother was insistent. She was convinced that I had appendicitis and she refused to allow me to use a hot water bottle to alleviate the excruciating pain I experienced the night of my final attack. Lucky for me! If I had used the water bottle, the pain may have subsided and I would have died, or become severely ill. For, sure enough, the appendix had ruptured that night, just as my mother knew it would.

* ✻ *If you have a memory of divine intervention, share it now. If you can't think of one in your own life, perhaps you have heard about something that happened to a friend, or of a story in the news. If you still can't think of one, keep your ears open. There's something magical about listening for stories recounting divine help. The more we look, the more often we become aware of it. Stories like these make us confront the truth of the old saying, "There but for the grace of God, go I."*

Come back to his page at any time to add divine interventions.

SAVORING

Chocolate Circles of Love
Leslie Brittman

For years I believed that the chocolate covered raspberry jelly was unique in the universe, the only candy endowed with magic. These candies mystically and instantly bestow unconditional love upon those who partake of the great pleasure of their taste.   This truth, as I believed it, was revealed to me at a very young age, in Brooklyn, at my great Aunt Rose's house. The time was the late forties and early fifties, when I was too young to realize the secrets I would unravel later as an adult - such as the fact that Aunt Rose's son Sussie had a real name, Sol. But the greatest secret of all was how those chocolate covered raspberry jellies worked their magic, each and every time, on every visit to my Great Aunt Rose.

Aunt Rose's house was a two story, but family life took place on the main level. The rooms were long, set out like blocks, one after another. First there was the porch. How I loved that porch! Things HAPPENED on that porch. That's where Sussie would take up his guitar, and the cousins would gather round and sing for hours. That's where one of the older cousins stole a kiss with her "beau" when she thought no one could see (but I saw!).   That's where I checked the seams on my nylon stockings, the first time I was grown up enough to wear them (to Aunt Rose's in Brooklyn!). And that's where my first love told me he loved me, when I was eleven.

At the back of the house was the kitchen, which was the first stop upon arriving (I would then work my way back to the front of the house, the porch). Apron-clad Aunt Rose would always be in the kitchen. Even when I was very small, Aunt Rose never seemed to be a large woman. In fact, she was tiny in stature, like a Jewish Mrs. Claus – soft, round, gray haired, with a kind smile and a soft touch. Her first hug and "look-over" were the beginning of her ritual of marveling. I got bigger, prettier, and smarter every time I came to see Aunt Rose.

After the initial hug and "look-over," I was on my own. I would go through the living/dining room on my way back to the porch. The chocolate covered raspberry jellies were always waiting for me in the same spot in the living room. Aunt Rose would always call out, "Take, take, shayna maydela, take as many as you like." The Yiddish "shayna maydela means "sweet girl."

When I sat down with those chocolate covered jellies, knowing that I could have as many as I wanted, I knew that those candies were magic. Nowhere else in my whole childhood could I have as many as I wanted of ANYTHING. Nowhere else did I feel so special, just KNOWING I could have as many as I wanted. Can you imagine? NO LIMITS. Where childhood is a place of constantly being taught what the limits are; here was one place where I ruled. I don't remember how many I ever ate. I just remember the feeling. How could anyone who had just been given rights to the whole dish of chocolate covered raspberry jellies be anything but invincible!

I had not thought much about Aunt Rose and her candy dish until recently, when I became a great aunt for the first time. Now, in adulthood, it's easy to see where the poor old candy dish would have been without Aunt Rose. So I have my candy dish waiting for Melanie, my great niece, and can't wait for her to be old enough to understand when I tell her, "take as many as you like, sweet girl." That, in your great aunt's house, you will know unconditional love.

How Can You Relate To This Story?

This story inspires in me such a wonderful feeling of being loved as well as the sense of delight about a special treat. As I read the story, memories of wonderful treats from my childhood came back to me. I can remember, as if it were yesterday, the lollipops that my mother and grandmother treated me to in St. Claire's Restaurant. The glass counter in the front of the store was filled with candies, smelling so good, I imagined heaven would smell like St. Claire's. But the ones I really wanted were the big giant lollipops on sticks in the shapes of toys. One was in the shape of a small locomotive; one was in the shape of a doll. Finally, one day, five in a box were purchased for me. I particularly enjoyed the lime flavor of the little choo-

choo train. I wanted it to last forever, and reading Leslie's story, it's as if it did.

Why don't you have some fun now, listing and remembering as many foods as you can that you love? Go for it. You're just writing them down so no calories are being ingested. I'll start you off.

* *Whole chunks of lobster in butter.*
* *Coffee ice cream with hot fudge.*
* *Hershey's candy bar.*
* *Homemade mashed potatoes.*
* _____
* _____
* _____

SHARING

The Lady and the Biscuits

Hilda, a young Jewish woman, made a last-minute airline reservation and rushed to the airport: her family, who lived across the country, had asked that she come as soon as possible. But no sooner did Hilda arrive at the terminal than she realized she hadn't brought any food for the trip. Because she kept kosher, this loomed as a huge problem.

Fortunately, she managed to find a package of kosher biscuits at a food shop. With some time before her flight, she decided to sit in the food court and have her biscuits. The area was extremely crowded and she was lucky to find a place to sit.

Within minutes, a man approached her to ask if he could share the table. She said yes, and he sat down opposite her. Absently, she took a biscuit from the package on the table. To her surprise, the man reached over and took a biscuit, too. She couldn't believe it! Not wanting to be rude, she didn't say anything; she just took another biscuit. The man did the same. Soon, only one was left. Smiling, the man reached for it, broke it two, and gave her half.

Hilda was furious. What kind of man was he anyway! Those were her biscuits! If he hadn't been so brazen, she might have offered him one. But instead of waiting, he had helped himself to half the bag. Now she had a long flight ahead of her, and she was still hungry.

Soon her flight was called. Hilda boarded the plane, found her seat, and proceeded to organize her things. When she opened her purse, there, to her amazement, was a full package of biscuits. Only then did she remember that she'd put the package in her purse when she sat down at the table. The biscuits she'd eaten hadn't been hers at all, but the mysterious man's. How generous he now seemed. He'd even shared the very last one with her.

How Can You Relate To This Story?

❋ Have you ever made negative assumptions about someone? Though they may be painful to recall, write them down here.

❋ Have you been surprised to later discover that the person was acting more in your best interest than you initially thought? How did you feel when you discovered your error? Describe the situation.

❋ What did you learn from the experience?

SINGING

A Brighter Day
Emily Doherty

I awoke one Saturday to a morning that reminded me of the lyrics to the famous song from "Oklahoma!" – "when the wind came right behind the rain." Determined, in true New England fashion, to ignore the forecast of an imminent hurricane, I left my husband to his rainy day Rip Van Winkle snoozing and went to look in on my daughter, also snoozing. But then I whispered the magic words in her ear: "Freehold Mall." Sure enough, a mere half-hour later she was in the shower, the sound of which woke Rip himself. Together with our other children, we piled in the car, determined to Enjoy Being A Family.

I winced a bit as my husband clicked on the car radio. It's not that I don't share his love of classical music, just that his taste can be a bit heavy for me. But to our mutual surprise, the local classical station was playing an unusual piece we both knew! In our pre-parental existence, we had both been singers; in fact, that experience had been the circumstance of our first meeting, a fact that was often obscured in the push and pull of everyday life.

The lyrical melody I heard on the radio instantly transported me to a magical morning some thirty years ago. Waking at 4:30 AM to find the Connecticut temperature maliciously hovering at 33 degrees, I had closed my overstuffed suitcase by sitting on it one more time, and then trekked bravely across the sodden campus, braving the first of the spring rains, to a gingerbread fraternity house. After drinking two cups of lukewarm leftover coffee I'd later regret, I threw my soggy trench coat over my new blue Villager suit, boarded the waiting bus, and headed with my fifty fellow choristers to the airport. We were greeted with fog – in the air, on the horizon, and in the glazed eyes of the frustrated commuters whose flights to Boston and Washington, DC had been indefinitely delayed. Combing the rain out of my hair, I took a seat in the airport's waiting room.

Suddenly, as if by magic, I found myself arm-in-arm with the other singers who would soon become my friends. In the fog of early morning, despite the delay and our mutual discontent, we began singing the first few haunting notes of the renaissance mass we had endlessly rehearsed. We weren't standing in our usual groupings – I rubbed elbows with basses, tenors, and altos – yet together we composed a morning miracle. Elegantly, our voices rose above the buzz of the restless crowd, silencing them with wonder. On the wings of our song, we left the waiting room behind and found ourselves in the vaulted arches of an ancient basilica.

The memory of what happened that morning permeated the tour we took together – two weeks of canons and camaraderie, never to be forgotten.

And that recent Saturday morning, in our car on the way to the Freehold Mall, the song on the car radio banished both the rain, winds and the weekend woes, becoming once again an instrument of enchantment. I felt good. I could see my husband smiling and relaxing as the children dozed. Yes, I was enjoying the moment, my family and my memories!

How Can You Relate To This Story?

So often in adult life, we awaken to a day filled with the prospect of chores and nuisance tasks, and feel overwhelmed with negative thoughts. And if the weather is bad, well, that's even worse! Emily's story gives us courage to try to rise above our immediate circumstances and look for positive cues, wherever we are.

One Saturday when I was about 16, I found myself in a despairing mood. I had no plans, no boyfriend, and nothing to look forward to. Even worse, my parents were going out, so I'd be alone in the house for the entire evening. I started to cry. My situation felt intolerable. In the midst of my tears, I remember crying out to God, "Please, let something good happen!"

Suddenly, the telephone rang. It was our new, very dear friends, Mr. & Mrs. Sylvester, who were in their seventies, calling to invite my parents to the theater with them. Seizing the moment, I told them that my parents were out and that I had no plans. Graciously, they asked if I'd like to join them at the theater instead. Now, 16 year old girls don't normally go out with a couple in their 70s. But for some reason, our age difference didn't matter. I felt my heart begin to pound with an unexpected eagerness. My prayers were answered. Not only was I going out on a Saturday night, but I was going to the theater, which I loved.

By the time Mr. and Mrs. Sylvester arrived to pick me up, I was dressed up and ready to go – and still elated. We attended a wonderful local production of "Blithe Spirit," one of the greatest Noel Coward plays that I've always enjoyed. I came home refreshed, tired – and convinced that a bad day can be transformed into a good one.

❋ Take some time now to reminisce. You, too, may remember a day that seemed filled with darkness but suddenly turned brighter. Recall that story now. If nothing comes to mind, don't worry. I guarantee that all you have to do is plant the seed. Once you believe that a bad day can turn good, you will discover that it actually happens.

SURVIVING

The Rabbi Who Lived in the Woods

There once was a Rabbi in training. His teacher usually held his lessons outdoors, where he would intersperse his scholarly talks with lessons about nature. His long white beard flowing and hands clasped behind his back, he would interrupt their walks, saying, "You see that mushroom? It's poisonous; don't ever eat it."

"*Why is he telling me this,*" his student would wonder. "*I never eat food that is lying around, my mother is a great cook and I am never hungry in her home.*"

On another walk the older man would point to the nearby fields. "Come and see, there are some herbs growing here. If you cut yourself, take the herbs and rub them into the wound, it will help them to heal." Again the student said to himself, "*Why does he tell me this? We have a doctor in the village; I go to him when I need medical assistance.*"

This went on for months and then years, the younger man's head bowed as he respectfully listened to his learned teacher, who always interrupted his Talmudic teachings with talks about how plants in the wilds could be used to a person's benefit.

One day a cloud came over the village: the Holocaust had reached the young Rabbi's village. Facing capture and the dreaded concentration camps that were

137

rumored to be the fate of the Jews, he fled into the forest. There he was able to live by eating the plants, shrubs, fruits and berries that his dear Rabbi had taught him would be safe to eat. When he suffered a cut or wound, he used the same herbs that he had been taught would make him well.

Not only did the young Rabbi's strong faith keep him alive, but all the things his old teacher had shown and taught him, when they had wandered together through the forest years before, came to his rescue and kept him alive. What had never seemed important to the young man thirsting for Biblical knowledge, served to save his life.

After the Holocaust ended, the young man went on to become a great, learned Rabbi, in his turn revered by those whose lives he touched.

We never know how important our learning may prove to be. We should savor all kinds of knowledge; you can never tell when one will become important later in life.

How Can You Relate To This Story?

* *Have you ever learned something that when you first started, it seemed purposeless and burdensome?*

I remember how terrible I felt when I first took typing. How boring the practice exercises were! Yet over the years, typing has proven to be one of my greatest assets, making it possible for me to keep notes and records on so much of both my personal and my professional life.

✸ *Can you reminisce about some form of learning that went from feeling irritating and annoying, to becoming a very positive, important part of your life? If you have a story from your life, write it down. If you can't think of one, just carry with you the memory of the Rabbi's walks in the forest. You never know when something you're asked to learn will someday result in enchantment rather than in frustration or annoyance.*

TRUSTING

The Hatpin

Rabbi Akiva lived during the 12th century and was considered one of the great scholars and leaders in Judaism. He had a daughter, and on the day she was born, a soothsayer told him that she would die on her wedding day, bitten on the arm by a poisonous snake. This is as tragic a fate as anyone can imagine – raising a daughter while worrying that you will lose her on what should be the most beautiful day of her life.

Rabbi Akiva decided not to believe the soothsayer, although he certainly thought about what she had said. But he trusted God, so he proceeded to make arrangements for his daughter's wedding. A proper suitor was found, and the wedding day soon arrived.

The daughter knew nothing of the strange prophecy, but she did have a terrible headache that day. Finally, unable to bear the headdress she was wearing, she took it off and absently stuck the large hatpin that held it into the edge of a curtain in her bedroom. Immediately, shaking and hissing sounds seemed to emanate from behind the curtain, but the daughter had already left the room.

The marriage ceremony took place as scheduled, followed by a daylong celebration and feast – and, indeed, to Rabbi Akiva's great relief, his daughter remained alive and well. The next day, the daughter remembered the hatpin and sent a servant to retrieve it from the curtain. As he wrenched it free, to his amazement, the servant heard a loud thud, as if something had fallen to the floor. Upon investigation, he discovered a poisonous dead snake on the floor behind the curtain. It bore a fatal wound along its side, apparently from being stabbed by the daughter's hatpin.

How Can You Relate To This Story?

I remember when my ballet teacher predicted to my mother that I would be too tall to become a professional dancer. Her prediction crushed my dreams in an instant. Now I would never become a professional dancer. I put aside my toe shoes and stifled my dreams. How ironic, given the fact that by the time I was an adult, many professional dancers were my height of 5' 8" or even taller.

* ❋ *Can you think of a time when a prediction got you in trouble? (Perhaps you became frightened or gave up on something?)*

❉ Did you ever feel you had been protected, or saved from harm, as Rabbi Akiva's daughter was from a disaster? Tell the story.

❉ Have you ever been able to override a prediction given to you, by sheer will, prayer, or belief in yourself? Tell the story.

VISITING

The Matzo Factory

From the outside, it looked like a decrepit old building. Perhaps a used furniture store or an old hardware store was concealed behind the wooden slats. Entering, I was amazed to see that the building was teeming with life.

First, I saw a room with long tables. Women wearing housedresses or full skirts and blouses, and kerchiefs around their heads reminiscent of the "old country," were busily making Passover matzo. They used long thin rollers similar to the rolling pin in my kitchen but three times as long and one third as thick. According to the tradition, they had to work quickly – they had only eighteen minutes to completely prepare and cook the matzo.

Watching the women, I felt energized, my positive energy level so palpable that I could taste it. Several of them smiled at me. I yearned to stay with them, to be taken in by them, given a housedress and a rolling pin and a spot at one of the tables. They were triggering some very old memories and feelings in me that had faded but not died, of being taken in by people and feeling safe. I would like to tell you about one of these memories.

I was visiting Joannie*, a college friend, who lived with her parents in a very small house that looked run-down by my suburban standards. Their living room contained stuffed old furniture. A dining room table and chairs were squeezed into one corner. The kitchen was terribly outdated – I didn't even see any appliances. That night I'd arrived, her mother, a voluminous woman, came to the door in a large print housedress, her hair messy, wearing no make-up. She gave me a big hug.

As we chatted and snacked, I realized that someone had put a record on.

Joannie was a violinist and I knew that her whole family loved music. Suddenly, Mrs. R. jumped up and started folk dancing all by herself, turning, bowing and spinning. The house was filled with warmth and energy. I loved watching her. Soon we were all moving and swaying. The rooms seemed to expand to hold our movements. Mrs. R. was a true ballerina of the soul!

When I left the next day, everything outside seemed cold and empty, almost sterile. I was confused by my reaction, the elation I had experienced in their house, and my desire to remain. Yet the house possessed none of the externals I had been taught to value. It wasn't clean, or roomy, and it didn't have a spacious new kitchen. Her mother wasn't thin and didn't wear make-up or stylish clothes. Joannie herself didn't even meet my standards! She was brainy, an attribute I admired, but plain – and eschewed make-up just as her mother did.

Years later, in a matzo factory watching Russian immigrants, (who had lived their lives unable to celebrate Passover), molding sacred Passover dough, creating a special positive energy system, I experienced a sense of welcoming comfort. I felt myself to be an integral part of things rather than standing apart from them. This feeling made colors richer. The external values to which I'd clung seemed to matter less.

As I watched the women, I knew in my soul that I was watching Joannie's mom. This wasn't the only time that I have felt elated, or excited, or really enjoyed myself, but the women in the matzo factory touched the deepest recess of my soul. The experience validated my belief in the human spirit. It was like walking into a well-defined room that felt as solid as a rock flooded with brilliant, transparent sunlight.

I couldn't bring myself to leave the matzo factory; I felt like a child who has to be dragged away from a beloved activity. Outside, I felt bereft. The sidewalk seemed cold and empty, as if the sun had set, though it was still shining. All of life seemed within that room, not out here. If I had been a little younger, maybe a little braver, I would have let the tears of soul knowledge pour down my face. Or I would have run back into the matzo factory, hugged one of the women and said, "Thank you for being here and embracing me with positive energies!" But I didn't have the courage. I went along with my day as best as I knew how, working as hard as I could to knead their sunlight into the bread of my life.

Yet I did have the courage to acknowledge a painful truth: that there had been many times in my life where I had lost a chance for enchantment because I clung to a set of notions, attitudes, or biases as to what was acceptable.

Much to my surprise, I'd seen that many chubby women in housedresses can lead exuberant lives filled with connection, warmth, and delight. At the same time, I had to acknowledge that many coiffured, thin women – women who look as if they have it all together – live lives of quiet despair and disappointment.

This ache in my heart signaled to me that I still had time – time to move beyond outmoded biases and trite notions about others. Although I didn't physically return to the matzo factory that day, metaphorically I walked out backwards, so that I could hold in my heart all the sunlight and joy that I had witnessed there and have it last for days and years to come.

*Name Changed

How Can You Relate To This Story?

✿ *Has there ever been a time in your life when you were startled by the intensity of joy and positive emotions you experienced? If so, write about that experience here.*

✻ Taking into account your own interests, talents, preferences, and potential, what are several activities that would elicit a sense of passionate connection and joy from you?

For example, because of my desires to belong, to be part of a community, to continue to learn, and to feel involved in something vital, I would love to embrace many new experiences. Here are two of them: to work in a community theater for a week so I could participate in a live performance; and to go to Israel to volunteer on a Kibbutz or in a hospital. Both of these opportunities intrigue me and set my pulse racing.

✻ I hope you'll take the time to reflect on activities that could potentially lead to your own Recipes for Enchantment. Over the next few months, come back to your notes, and see if one or more of your ideas stands out from the others.   Perhaps it's time to try to make at least one fantasy a reality.

WALTZING

Grandfather Really Knew How to Dance!

My friend Mary Ellen recently began taking ballroom dancing lessons through a local adult education program. As she relaxes in the strong arms of her teacher, a courtly gentleman who is teaching her to fox trot, cha-cha and tango, Mary Ellen's memories return to her first dancing partner, her grandfather.

When she was a girl, she took several ocean voyages to Europe with her grandparents on the Queen Elizabeth II. Her grandfather, she tells me, looked like a Spanish count, and not without reason – the blood of Spanish royalty ran in his veins. Yet he always acted like the perennial host, welcoming people and treating everyone like royalty.

What she remembers best are the formal evening activities. She loved getting ready for dinner – slipping into her taffeta dresses and satiny, shiny shoes. They were enough to make any awkward, homely, eleven-year-old girl feel as if she'd stepped into a fairy tale.

But the dressing up was only a part of the fun. Best of all was when her tall, distinguished, perpetually tanned grandfather would take her in his arms. Gliding with him across the polished dance floor with the live orchestra playing behind them, she felt transformed. No longer chubby and insecure, she was now a beautiful woman, a svelte princess. It was an ENCHANTED MOMENT.

For a long time, Mary Ellen thought those elegant days were gone forever. But when she began taking dance lessons, she was flooded with memories – of the ship, the music, her imagined beauty, and most of all, of her grandfather. Now she finds herself enjoying ENCHANTED MOMENTS in her everyday life, reinforced by her memories from so long ago.

How Can You Relate To This Story?

❋ *Think of all your activities. Is it possible that you could derive more pleasure from them than you now do, if you associated them with pleasant memories? To find out, pick an activity you already enjoy. Close your eyes and let your mind wander. Think of times in the past when you enjoyed this or similar activities. Write your memories here.*

✼ Can you recall any pleasant memories that would be rekindled if you embarked upon a similar activity now, just as Mary Ellen's dance lessons rekindled hers? What activity from your long-ago life could you bring back to life today? What great memory accompanies that activity? How would you go about including this activity in your present life?

There are always two ways to take advantage of your memories: by letting experiences from the past lead you to new ones, or by augmenting present-day activities with memories from the past. Don't forget: we are not simple. In our "Recipes for Enchantment," we enhance our activities with positive feelings and thoughts. The more positive threads we bring to the loom, the richer the tapestry, and the more we get out of enchanted living.

WELCOMING

A Familiar Friend
Doreen Laperdon-Addison

Caught up in the hustle and bustle of everyday life, I realize that it's been a long while since I've spent an extended period of time with a familiar friend – myself. Living often lends itself to excuses for not catching up with old acquaintances.

The summer of 1997 was great, the best in years. I've deposited in my personal memory bank enchanted recollections of going to the beach, swimming, hiking, taking day trips to museums and the zoo, and spending quality time with family and friends.

But the summer also summoned anxiety and restlessness on a deep personal level. During this time, I returned my focus to T'ai C'hi. I hadn't practiced it for about a year and a half. When I stopped, I knew that I would resume at some point. As time went on, though, I found myself worrying about all I had forgotten, which made it harder for me to begin again. But a dancer's mind also resides in her body (some people refer to this as "muscle memory"). When I first began practicing I was a little rusty, but found myself moving nonetheless. After a few weeks, I met with Peter Eno, my T'ai C'hi instructor and friend. With Peter, I realized how much I missed this type of movement, and the physical and emotional and spiritual pleasure I derive from it.

Establishing time for practice required that my whole family adjust its schedule. Initially I would practice in the house, trying to create a peaceful environment among people whose needs sometimes conflicted with mine. This proved difficult. I would imagine my husband thinking, "What is she up to now?" - while my daughter was shouting, "Where's Mommy?" But I continued. I couldn't deny that moving again made me breathe more deeply and feel both more relaxed and alert. Though this wasn't a formal "dance class," I was maintaining my flexibility while working on balance and other subtle movement patterns.

One morning, I found myself thinking that I should go outside and practice. I still remember gazing through the multi-colored leaves at the bluer-than-blue sky. Since then I've practiced outdoors every morning, regardless of the weather.

Why? My answer is simple: because it is exhilarating. My senses have become more attuned. Moving in this way enables me to reconnect with a friend: myself. Through my practice, I am learning how to maintain my focus on the present moment. I am also reminded of my love of learning and of nature, and of the importance of movement in my life. With childlike wonder I watch spiders spinning their webs, feel the sunshine on my skin, listen to the wind, and notice the squirrels, flowers, trees and vegetables while smelling the fragrant air.

My memories ebb and flow from past to present, creating the positive links that ground and support me as I continue to grow and change. My restlessness and anxiety have decreased. I now look forward to each morning, when I move, sometimes like a dancer and sometimes not, attuning myself to the rhythms within and without.

Welcome back, old friend. It's good to be on intimate terms once again.

How Can You Relate To This Story?

Sandwiched between family, work, and social obligations, we have so little time for ourselves. But you can take a few seconds or minutes out from your busy day anywhere, at any time. Here's a way to help welcome back your old friend.

The next time you walk to your car, cook a meal, or find yourself pushing your toddler on the swing at the playground, take a moment and say to yourself, "Stop!" Take a few deep breaths, and look at the world around you as if you just returned from a long trip. Notice the colors and smells that surround you, and the way the light plays with the leaves or your child's hair. Become aware of the temperature and the breeze. If you're sitting on a bench or waiting for a bus, study the people walking by. Notice how differently they move and dress. Listen for the sound of birds, or pay attention to the different sounds that the traffic makes. If you're in your kitchen, consider the colors that surround you, the view from your window, the taste and textures of the foods in your pantry and refrigerator, and the sounds of your settling house.

There are many ways to be "in the moment," attuned to your surroundings.   Experiencing yourself as an integral part of your environment will help you feel more relaxed and more positive about yourself. Paying attention to yourself in this way can help to bring you more in tune with your *ENCHANTED SELF*.

❋ *Write some notes here about an "in the moment" experience.*

WISHING

A Vision

   I see them coming onto the field knowing the land and knowing nature and knowing how to survive. They are strong and they know how to create a world. I see them in a giant circle holding hands - so many different peoples. The Amish and the Mennonites merge into the New England farmers, and they merge into the pioneers who crossed the country, and they merge into all the immigrants from the small villages in Europe. And then behind them I see another giant circle and that circle has tribal peoples from around the world and they too are holding hands. There are Native American Indians and Eskimos and people from high in the Andes. There are people out of Africa dancing in their tribal costumes and colorations. And in the middle is a giant bonfire. The stars are out and every one is singing joyful songs. And I walk amongst them and I'm holding on to the hands of people I love, and they are holding onto the hands of people they love, and we are making a giant chain of people that weaves its way in and out of these two circles.

   I'm never afraid. I realize that I have with me all of my family and friends and that I'm weaving in and out of all the groups, the courageous groups and tribes of the world. We are dancing in and out and circling around these people, and sometimes presents are given to us. Sometimes a feather is given to me or one of my family members or friends, or a piece of ribbon or some other treasure as we pass by. A barrette may be placed in my hair or a piece of paper with a note on it placed in my waistband. These I have time to relish later, but for the moment it is more important to be in motion and feel our bodies moving and hear the songs coming through. Soon we go inside and make a circle inside the first circle and we dance our own dance; all my friends and family and the dance just free flows. It works, and before we know it, we are all singing each of us and all the songs that come up into the sky are from each person's soul and they blend and harmonize.

Suddenly, I notice that the dawn is starting and the bonfire is going out. Just the embers are left, but the sun is coming up. Yes, we danced the whole night and the sky is now clearing, the sun is rising and it is this kind of wildness, a freedom, a sense of ecstasy is building at the same time as the fatigue is setting in. The air is so clean and the sky so clear and the darkness as it leaves is replaced by such a promise of a blue sky. And I'm aware that all the songs of each person's souls are filling the dawn. Can you imagine this field with a thousand people singing their song of their souls? And we all harmonize!

How Can You Relate To This Story?

* What's a dream of yours for mankind?

* A wish?

* A blessing you'd like to give to others?

CONCLUSION

"Always remember:
Joy is not merely incidental to
Your spiritual quest.
It is vital."

Rebbe Nachman of Breslov

Dear Readers:

I hope these stories that I have shared with you will become good companions as you journey through daily living. Each story, like any good friend, has its own disposition and style. Likewise, the activities that follow each story take you to different places and stretch you in different ways.

And as with good friends, there is always some work involved in getting the most out of the opportunity presented. I hope that your mental perspiration as you responded and shared your own feelings, thoughts, and stories was far outweighed by your inspiration. I hope you experienced a sense of purpose and joyfulness by taking this shared journey.

Remember, that above all, you are the secret ingredient in creating a life that is filled with positive actions and experienced as joyful and above all, unique to you.

I wish you wonderful adventures, pleasures beyond counting, and most of all I wish that every day of your life, you feel centered, whole, and that being YOU is the most fabulous adventure of all. Let this adventure resonate with the Divine. I wish for you that if you could be in touch with the celestial angels, you would hear them sing in harmony with you, your very own song.

Please send your stories of enchanted living with or without follow-up activities to: Dr. Barbara Becker Holstein, PO Box 2112, Ocean, NJ 07712, or submit them directly to encself@aol.com.

REFERENCES

Believing, Joey Figures It Out

Many thanks to Rabbi Joseph Friedman Temple Beth Torah, Wanamassa, NJ Your sermon last year inspired me to adapt a version of the story you told about a little boy who got better.

Discovering, The Mysterious Rabbi

Many thanks to the various books I have had a chance to read about the Mussar movement. This story was loosely adapted from one of the books. Unfortunately, I cannot find the book. If and when it does cross my path, I will reference it in future editions of RECIPES FOR ENCHANTMENT.

Pretending, The Claydigger Finds a Diamond

This story is loosely based on a story of Rabbi Nachman. One version of the story appears in <u>Under the Table and How to Get Up: Jewish Pathways of Spiritual Growth,</u> Avraham Greenbaum, TSOHAR Publishing (Jerusalem/New York, 1991), pp 205-208.

Sharing, The Lady and the Biscuits

This story has been making the rounds in Jewish learning circles for several years now, teaching a positive lesson.

Surviving, The Rabbi Who Lived in the Woods

This story is loosely based on a true story shared at a Shabbos table that I was privileged to be the guest at, in Lakewood, NJ.

CONTRIBUTING WRITERS

Becker, Bernice – BELONGING-When Saturday Was Really Saturday

Becker, Bernice – LAUGHING – How Could Timmie Disappear?

Brittman, Leslie – SAVORING – Chocolate Circles of Love

Doherty, Emily – SINGING – A Brighter Day

Hoyer, Bernadette – GRIEVING – Memories, Grieving and Resolution

Laperdon-Addison, Doreen – WELCOMING – A Familiar Friend

Rosen, Sherri – LIVING – Life At A Dharma Center: Challenging, Rewarding, and Not Easy!

Saposnik, Ellen – LOVING – Grandma Sadie's Blintzes

Schultz Margolin, Sylvia – REMINISCING – Not The Same Old Story

Singer, Tzvia – MENTORING – The Sweet Touch of Mr. Zuckerman

Wintram, Claire – DANCING – Dancing the Sardana

RECIPES FOR ENCHANTMENT, The Secret Ingredient Is YOU!

❀ ❀ ❀ ❀ ❀ ❀ ❀ ❀ ❀

Story Contest

Share with us your RECIPE FOR ENCHANTMENT. Dr. Holstein invites you to submit your own story of magic meaning and purpose. Dr. Holstein will select one special, amazing story as the contest winner. The winner will receive five (5) free copies of RECIPES FOR ENCHANTMENT, The Secret Ingredient is You! All successful runners up will receive one copy of RECIPES FOR ENCHANTMENT, The Secret Ingredient is You! Plus all entries will be considered for Volume II. Send your Recipes for Enchantment to Dr. Barbara Becker Holstein, PO Box 2112, Ocean, NJ 07712 or send them directly via e-mail to encself@aol.com.

To stay involved with Enchantment, subscribe to Enchantment in an E-mail via www.enchantedself.com or write to Dr. Holstein at encself@aol.com. Type "Subscribe" in the Subject line.

~~~~~~

Dr. Barbara Becker Holstein is available for media interviews, teleconferences, and hands on workshops, lectures and life coaching. She can be reached at 1-877-BJOYFUL. Her website is www.enchantedself.com and her e-mail address is encself@aol.com.

About the Author

Dr. Barbara Becker Holstein is a nationally known leader in Positive Psychology. Her first book, THE ENCHANTED SELF, A Positive Therapy, challenged outdated psychological behaviors and attitudes. It taught clinicians and the public how to recognize what is right about each of us rather than what is wrong. Her emphasis on positive memory retrieval profoundly changed the focus of the treatment room. Now we can joyfully reclaim our talents and lost potential, even from a dysfunctional past.

Joy and discovering our purpose in life are essential to all of Dr. Holstein's teachings. She educates the public in ways to increase the joy in one's life. She eagerly shares her knowledge with the public via her constant radio and television appearances. Also, her newsletters go around the world both via the post and e-mail. Her website, www.enchantedself.com , is a clearing house of good news and learning opportunities. The public can go to this site to practice enchantment while reading positive stories from readers around the world.

Dr. Holstein knows that practice is essential to live a life of joy and meaning. Thus, she gives the reader the opportunity to use each story in RECIPES FOR ENCHANTMENT, The Secret Ingredient is YOU! as a springboard for the enticing soul searching necessary to become in touch with one's unique gifts and how best to use them, thus creating the personal "magic" of an enchanted life.

Dr. Barbara Becker Holstein is available for media interviews, teleconferences, and hands on workshops, lectures and life coaching. She can be reached at 1-877-BJOYFUL. Her website is www.enchantedself.com and her e-mail address is encself@aol.com.